children's
Parties

children's Parties

Planning Unique and Unforgettable Parties For Your Child

Juliette Rogers
Barbara Radcliffe Rogers

PRICE STERN SLOAN

Los Angeles

A TERN ENTERPRISES BOOK

© 1990 by Tern Enterprises, Inc.

Published by Price Stern Sloan, Inc.
360 North La Cienega Boulevard, Los Angeles, California 90048

Printed in Hong Kong.
1 3 5 7 9 8 6 4 2

LIBRARY OF CONGRESS CATALOGING-IN-PUBLICATION

Rogers, Barbara Radcliffe.
　　Children's parties / by Barbara Radcliffe Rogers and Juliette
Rogers.
　　　　p.　cm.
　　Includes index.
　　ISBN 0-89586-783-4 : $24.95—ISBN 0-89586-811-3 (pbk.) : $12.95
　　1. Children's parties.　I. Rogers, Juliette.　II. Title.
GV1205.R57 1989
793.2′1—dc19　　　　　　　　　　　　　　　　　89-3602
　　　　　　　　　　　　　　　　　　　　　　　CIP

CHILDREN'S PARTIES
Planning Unique and Unforgettable Parties for Your Child
was prepared and produced by
Tern Enterprises, Inc.
15 West 26th Street
New York, New York 10010

Editor: Stephen Williams
Designer: Judy Morgan
Art Director: Robert W. Kosturko
Senior Photography Editor: Christopher Bain
Photography Editor: Ede Rothaus
Production Manager: Karen L. Greenberg

Back cover/jacket photo by Tony Freeman/PhotoEdit
Cover/jacket design by Judy Morgan

Typeset by Mar + x Myles Graphics, Inc.
Color separations by United South Sea Graphic Art Co., Ltd.
Printed and bound in Hong Kong by South China Printing Co. Ltd.

DEDICATION

For Lura, whose advice on every detail has been invaluable. After all, who would know better than an eleven-year-old what kinds of parties kids love best?

© Robert Kaufman/Silver Visions Publishing Co.

© Jay Brenner/FPG International

CONT

SECTION II
Unique Children's Parties
38

© Tom Stack/Tom Stack & Associates

© Jeffry W Myers/FPG International

E N T S

INTRODUCTION

Party! You don't have to be a kid to be excited by that word. But for a child, the word party is magic. It gives rise to thoughts of cake and ice cream, games, presents and bright decorations.

A birthday or holiday is always an occasion to anticipate, and planning for a party just compounds the excitement. A child's first parties are usually family ones—christenings and birthday celebrations where the child is the star, but adults are the real guests. Even for a toddler, a party is more likely to be a gathering of grandparents and aunts and uncles than of other young friends, so plan accordingly.

As the child grows, parties take on a more social aspect. Young friends gather to play exciting games and decorations are planned just for the children.

But good parties don't just happen. Behind every party there is a parent, grandparent, older brother, sister or friend who planned it all. Throwing a party doesn't have to be a tremendous task; in fact, it can be one of the most rewarding experiences possible.

This book gives you a lot of traditional party ideas. But since a party is more than decorations and games, this unique guidebook helps you plan the most important party ingredient—the guest list.

The party giver must keep in mind both the needs of the guest of honor and the guests. An exciting afternoon of new people and new games may sound like fun to adults, but children prefer things that are comfortable. A birthday party for preschoolers, for example, is not the place to teach a new game, unless it is a very simple one. The children will be very excited, and the listening skills they are just developing might be switched off for the afternoon.

Instead, start with things they all know—familiar games, popular songs or activities that use skills the children already have. Remember that this will be the first time many of the kids have visited your home, so look for something fun to do that will also make them feel at ease.

The same cautionary note applies to food. For youngsters, familiar foods are best. Because young children might be edgy from the excitement of the occasion, and young tastes vary, stick to foods that everyone knows. (Almost every child loves peanut butter and jelly sandwiches.) Try your hand at presenting the old standbys in new and amusing ways, but save the exotic delights for adults.

In choosing a theme, remember the age and stage of development of the children who will be there. A Roman toga party might be great fun for college fraternities, but its meaning will be lost on first graders. Stick to themes that can be under-

stood by those attending the party. The most important thing to remember is that parties are fun, and having fun is more important than following a strict party plan.

To use this book, first skim through the pages and look at the boxes that accompany each party plan. These will help you determine if the activities and themes fit your child's age group. Make sure you can meet the requirements for space or supplies. And decide whether or not the idea sounds like fun for you and your child.

After you've chosen a specific party theme, be sure to browse through the others as well, since many ideas are interchangeable. See the games on pages 34 to 37, for activities that will suit the children who will be at the party. Mix and combine them with your own ideas and those of your child to create an original party. Chances are, it will be the subject of happy memories for everyone involved—including you!

S E C T I O N

1

Hosting the Perfect Party

Planning a Party

PARTY PLANNING LIST

Date and time

Reservations made (if necessary)

Theme

Guest list made

Number of guests

Invitations made or bought

Invitations sent

Decorations planned

Materials needed for decorations

Supplies needed (paper plates, etc.)

Supplies purchased

Favors and prizes purchased

Refreshments planned

Caterer or baker contacted

Ingredients to purchase

Decorations made

Games and activities planned

Materials for games/activities to purchase

Food prepared and ready

Decorations in place

The first step in planning a party is to set a time and place—and since the theme may well be involved in this decision, you should also think about the type of party to have.

After you've chosen a theme, a time and a place, draw up a guest list. The number of children, their ages and their interests will influence your plans for activities, games and even decorations.

The next step is writing invitations. They should hint at the kind of party you're throwing. Send them out at least two weeks in advance, and be sure to ask the invited guests to respond so you know how many children will be attending.

Decorations depend on the theme and occasion, and since some may take a little effort, you will need to consider them early. Favors and prizes may also fit into your theme. Give yourself enough time to find them.

Refreshments are always important, and although you shouldn't make them too far in advance, you should consider what to buy and how much preparation time you'll need. If you're using a bakery or caterer, don't wait until the last minute to make the arrangements.

You may find it handy to fill out and tape a copy of the checklist to your bulletin board while you are getting ready for the party.

The Guest List

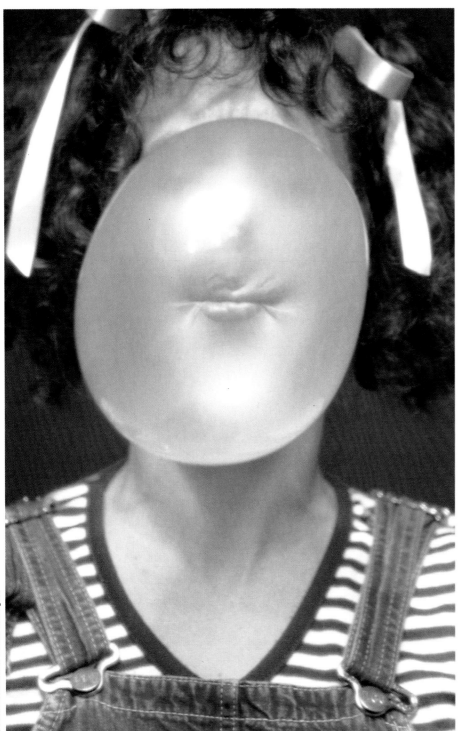

The choice of whom to invite to the party should be the child's. Discuss this carefully with him or her and set a limit on the number of kids that can be invited. Except for very young children, kids have pretty good instincts about who likes whom and how a group will get along. Your child will express certain preferences, but be sure these are not based on who he or she just had a fight with. Children's social ties tend to change more frequently than those of adults. The guest list is a matter to discuss over a period of a few days.

Just because your best friend's or boss' children are the same age as yours, don't assume that your child wants to invite them. Don't make the birthday child responsible for playing host to a child the others don't know, unless it is the child's idea.

Likewise, if your child wants to add someone not known by the rest of the group, discuss this as well. Will the new child feel comfortable? Are the other children who are invited usually quick to accept someone new into their group?

If the party guests do not know each other, plan a few get-acquainted games (see pages 34 to 37) and activities that don't involve selecting partners or teams.

13

The Right Party for Your Child

Here's what to expect of children at various ages:

Toddlers, age 1 to 3: Social instincts are not well honed at this age, although older toddlers may be able to play well with others. This is a time for very small groups of children, (five to eight kids), very short parties and very simple activities. Expect (and ask) parents to stay with their child unless you know the child well. Extra adults are a must at parties for the very young.

At this age it is not a good idea to bring together a large group of children who do not know each other. A play group or a few children from the same day-care class make a good group. Play needs to be supervised at all times and the area of activity should be fairly limited. Games should be ones all the children already know. Simple repetitive singing games are popular with kids this age. Ask their day-care teacher to suggest games they know.

Keep parties for this age group short, and have them in the morning, if possible. Be sure to have a toy or game that will involve all the children at once, and do not put your child in the position of having to suddenly share all his toys. This is an age where sharing skills are still being learned, and it isn't fair to expect too much all at once, even if your child has been very willing to share with playmates in the past.

Preschoolers, age 3 to 5: At this age children begin to enjoy each other as playmates and they play together instead of playing individually in a group. (No more than ten children should be invited.) They begin to discover group activities and react well to the give-and-take of playing. But these skills are still not something you can take for granted, so children of this age should have well-planned activities at a party.

Games can be a little more complicated and use the children's developing motor skills. Be sure to keep activities easy enough to include those children who are slower to develop, since there may be wide variations in skills among children of the same age.

At this age boys and girls still play together in groups, and love dressing up and active play, like using hand puppets. Good supervision from you and a few extra adults is still necessary. Although more children can be invited at this age, don't invite a very large group unless all the children are used to being together in class, at a play group or somewhere else.

New-schoolers, age 5 to 6: More advanced in social skills, children of this age are in school or preparing for it, and are very good at making friends. They may enjoy a slightly less structured party with a little free playtime at the end. They are beginning to develop individual interests, but these are likely to be similar to their friends'— dinosaurs, space travel, Native Americans and science and history are popular with this age group. Since they have more physical control, games of skill such as those in the Olympics party are a good idea. So are simple craft activities. Depending on their particular social habits,

14

the children may prefer to be in groups of all boys or all girls. (Six to ten children is a good number to invite.)

Primary school, age 6 to 8: At this age children have a longer attention span, which makes more complicated games and activities possible. They are developing physical skills that give them better aim and coordination, and like to play games of skill. Counting games are fun for these kids. Nonsense rhymes—the sillier the better—are also great favorites, so go wild with scavenger hunt clues. They love the sound of words, so reading a story aloud or playing a recording is a good way to settle them down. Primary-school children like storybook characters, dressing up, acting in plays and informal, unstructured play. (Invite no more than ten to fifteen children of this age for a good party.)

Preteens, age 9 to 12: Although there is a great variety of development within this group, one common thread holds them together: These children are beginning to grow up, and like to be treated, at least socially, as adults. But they still need guidance, support and leadership. They do not like to look like children, but they still enjoy children's games and activities once they get caught up in the excitement. Children of this age are characterized by great bursts of physical energy—this is important to remember, especially if the party is after school, when they've been on their best behavior all day and need to let off some steam. Games should involve active participation, but can also involve mental challenges—treasure and scavenger hunts with riddle clues are good choices. (Between ten and twenty-five guests is a good number for these parties.)

Preteens are often antagonistic toward the opposite sex, even though they are beginning to be attracted to them, so it is better to keep parties separate at this age unless there is a coed group that is used to being together socially, such as a neighborhood, church, sports or hobby group.

Offer activities that allow the guests to succeed, but that aren't too competitive. Self-confidence is a rare commodity in this group and failure can be crushing, so look for games where everyone is a winner. Free time for unstructured play is a good idea, but be ready with an activity in case it doesn't work well.

Your Child as Guest

When your child receives an invitation to a party, be sure that you read it, noting details and adding them to your calendar. If the child is too young to respond, be sure to do so yourself.

If this is your child's first party, be sure to talk about what to expect and how to act. This is also a good time to discuss a gift, if one is appropriate, so that your child feels part of this decision. One of the best ways to find good gifts is to shop with your child—then you can agree on a gift that is attractive to a child and acceptable to parents. Your own child's wish list is a good place to find ideas for other kids the same age. If possible, have your child wrap the present.

Be prompt, and take your child to the door so the host can meet you if you don't already know each other. If your child is very young, offer to stay and help, and leave a telephone number where you can be reached. Be there at the appointed time or a few minutes early to pick up your child. Don't be late.

© Stephen McBrady/PhotoEdit

16

Challenged Children

Often parents feel uncomfortable or unprepared when physically or mentally challenged children are guests at their party. But there's really no need to worry, and there probably won't be many adjustments to make. Of course, you can always speak with the child's parents if you feel you need some special advice. But chances are that the parent will inform you ahead of time if there is anything special you need to know.

Otherwise, just follow these tips offered by Easter Seals to make children more aware of the needs of physically and mentally challenged children. And make sure your child also understands this advice.

■ Don't be afraid to help someone, but don't just jump right in. Ask first, or wait for the child to request it.

■ Be aware that just because a child is in a wheelchair, doesn't mean that he is sick. Lots of people who are otherwise healthy and strong have to use wheelchairs for various reasons.

■ It's easier for everyone concerned if you sit down when you are talking to a person in a wheelchair, so you're both on the same level.

■ Go ahead and use words like "see," "hear," "walk" and "run" when you're talking to someone who can't do these things. The child will understand what you're talking about, and really, it's more unnatural to always try to avoid these words than it is to use them.

■ In the same vein, it's all right to ask people with speech impediments to repeat themselves.

© Raymond Stott/The Image Works

■ If a guest is using an interpreter, be sure to talk directly to the deaf person, not the interpreter.

■ Don't speak loudly when talking to blind people. They hear as well as you do.

■ Feel free to invite friends with disabilities to sleep over, play games or do other party activities. But think about ways to include them in what you do. When you are planning an activity, ask yourself if you would be able to do it if you were challenged in the same way as your guest.

Handmade Invitations

The invitation is the first news of a party. Its very arrival is an event. Even if the invitations can be passed out at school, mailing them gives them a special significance, and saves hurt feelings if the whole class is not invited. Since parties are always a topic of conversation at school, you may want to prepare your child for dealing with classmates who are not invited. Tell him to be truthful. He can say "My mother said I could only invite the three friends I play with most," or, "Since we're going on a trip, my mother wanted to invite only the kids whose mothers she knows." Try to give your child an answer for questions other kids will ask, before they ask them.

Invitations set the tone for the party well in advance. Along with telling the time, place and occasion, the invitation may give a hint of the excitement to come—big game footprints might suggest a jungle party, grinning clowns a circus theme. Offer helpful details about costumes and what to bring.

With a little help your school-aged child can make the invitations, either by drawing designs on the front or using some of the many colorful stickers available in card and stationery stores. If you would rather buy invitations, you will find a variety of ready-made ones suitable for all ages.

Day. Depending on their ages, many children enjoy doing this part themselves.

Have the envelopes ready before making the cards—it's a lot easier to make cards to fit envelopes than the other way around! Don't worry if the handmade invitations don't look like the ones in the card shop—this is a time for the little host or hostess to be creative. The homemade look adds a special touch to each invitation that the other kids will appreciate.

A unique way to begin the party fun and surprises early is to write the invitations on jigsaw puzzle stationery. It comes in several colors with matching envelopes; you can write all the information on the puzzles and then have your child take them apart. Instead of a card, the addressee

The basic information to include on any invitation is the name of the host or hostess, the occasion, the date, the time, the place and RSVP information such as a telephone number. You may also want to give directions to the party and notes on anything special the guest should bring, such as clothes or a sleeping bag.

If you are making the invitations, you can use plain white paper or colored cards, which can be purchased by the box with matching envelopes. Or cut cards from colored art or construction paper in appropriate shapes, such as jack-o'-lanterns for Halloween or hearts for Valentine's

receives an envelope full of puzzle pieces to put together before the message is clear.

For a magic party, consider writing the invitations in invisible ink. Buy cheap pen points and holders at a stationery store, and write the invitations on paper using lemon juice instead of ink. Enclose a note written in regular ink telling the recipient to hold the paper near a hot light bulb for a moment to reveal the message.

If you or your child is clever with verse—or even if you're not clever, but just want to have fun—try writing a simple invitation poem, perhaps based on a familiar nursery rhyme.

Whatever form your invitation takes, it will be the highlight of someone's day.

These unusual invitations include (on the opposite page) a handmade valentine, and (this page) paper mittens, a felt party hat and bats made from construction paper.

Favors and Prizes

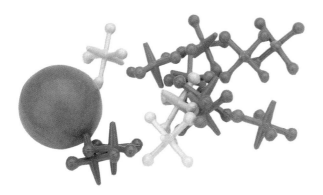

Everybody should leave a party with something, whether it is a prize won at a game or a special party favor. Sometimes you give these out as everyone leaves; other times you write the children's names on them and put them on the table as place cards. There are games—such as treasure hunts and spiderwebs (see pages 34 to 36)—which have prizes for everyone, based on completing the game, and not on speed, skill or chance.

Favors are usually very small things—pencils with animal or dinosaur erasers, stickers, balls and jacks, bags of marbles or other toys. These are usually inexpensive items, but they do not need to be worthless things that will easily break or just be thrown away after the first use. The trend today is away from candy as the standard party favor. Useful things like fancy erasers, cute little notebooks or crayons are sometimes better than toys.

Even the grocery store or pharmacy can be a good source of favors. Look for sample sizes of shampoo, bubble bath, hair conditioner and other toiletries.

You may also choose to have the guests make their own favors in a valentine-making party or a gingerbread Christmas party.

An excellent source of inexpensive but unique favors and prizes is the gift shop of a local children's or science museum. Irresistible treasures abound there—from polished stones to petrified shark teeth. A good way to assemble favors is to collect them over a period of time instead of shopping for them all at once in a party store.

Here is another place your child can have fun planning the party—ask advice on what to give for favors or take your child with you when you shop. You'll be surprised at some of the unusual

ALLOSAURUS

ideas that will turn up as you wander through a stationery store or other place you would normally consider a grown-up's domain.

A novel way to present party favors is to wrap them up in a ball of streamers. You can buy rolls of decorating streamers at party supply stores.

Wrap a small favor, such as a top or a ball, in the streamer as though you were starting a ball of yarn. Continue wrapping, adding in other small favors such as stickers, jacks, wrapped candies or novelty erasers. The ball can be as large as your patience allows.

Tie bows around the completed balls. Use these as table favors or pass them out as the children arrive. Be sure everyone has a small bag to collect the favors in as they unwrap them.

Great party prizes include (moving clockwise from the ball and jacks on the opposite page) tops, marbles, colored pencils, spiral-art tools, colored rocks and sunglasses.

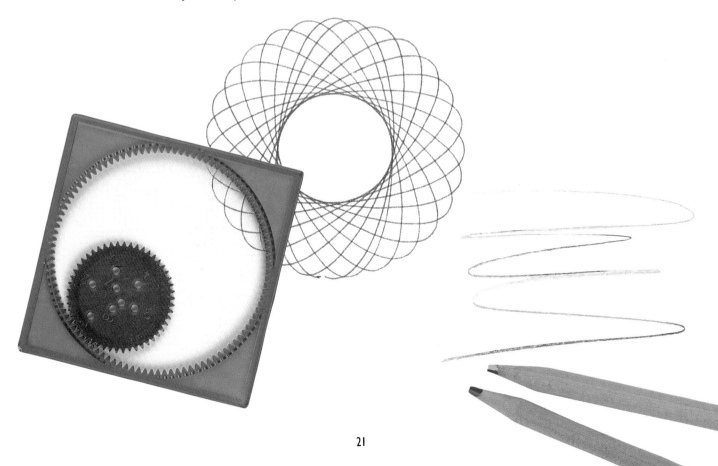

Party-Proofing Your House

You may need to protect your home against the mishaps that often occur when children are excited, especially if your party is for young children. It is better to be overcautious than to chance ruining the party for yourself or a guest by having some fragile treasure crash to the floor. A new stain on an Oriental carpet can spoil everyone's fun.

First decide which rooms you want to use for the party. Then take all the fragile items out of them. If there will be food or drink in a room, you may want to protect the upholstered furniture or expensive carpets from excited, food-bearing children by rolling back area rugs and covering the furniture with bright throws. Plastic dropcloths covered by colorful paper tablecloths can protect surfaces from damage, and make cleanup faster in case of spills. Small pieces of furniture can be removed entirely, leaving more room for the merry-making.

If party-proofing your home is not possible or practical, consider having the party elsewhere. YMCAs, gymnastics schools, private clubs and even restaurants have facilities for parties. Sometimes they will even help you with the planning and details. And, best of all, neither you nor the children will have to worry about ruining an expensive or cherished household item.

You can take steps to avoid accidents like this; help your child write thank you notes when the party is over (opposite page).

© Christopher Bain

Thank-You Notes

Writing thank-you notes for gifts is truly a wonderful custom that every child should adopt. The day after a birthday party is a good time to introduce a child to this social grace. Thank-you notes are often neglected, probably because they are thought of as a chore. But they can be fun if you give your child small cards—only a few words are necessary—and a selection of colorful stickers to use to decorate them. Choosing just the right sticker for each friend, or combining them to make a picture, will make the chore a game, and teach your child a valuable social skill at the same time. If your child is too young, write the message yourself.

Making a Memory Book

© George Goodwin

Looking back on past celebrations can be almost as much fun as planning and having the parties. The pictures of everyone playing games, copies of cute thank-you notes, handmade invitations and other mementos are as much fun for the child as they are for you, so be sure to keep souvenirs and take plenty of pictures.

If you plan to keep a memory book of parties and celebrations, there are things you will certainly want to include from each one. Always keep an extra invitation. You may want to include a short write-up on the planning, the menu, the decorations, the guest list and funny or outstanding events.

If it was a gift-giving occasion, note the gifts received. The food, the decorations and the children involved should be remembered in photographs. Casual shots are the most interesting to look back on—Sally emerging from the basin with an apple in her mouth; Tom pinning the tail squarely on the donkey's nose.

Photography shouldn't interrupt a party, but you can make it part of the fun. Make the guests the important "stars" of the event. Come in close

and get the faces of the children, rather than focusing on a roomful of people. Be prepared for the special moments—when the birthday girl blows out the candles or opens the special gift from grandpa.

The story of the party can be told in pictures alone, but captions make a memory book even more fun. For a special perspective you will both treasure in years to come, have your child help you with these. Instead of the traditional black-paged photo albums, try using a bound blank book with white paper. Cut every other page out with a single-edged razor blade one-fourth inch from the binding. This will leave you with half as many pages but twice as much space, to compensate for the bulk of the added photos and keep the binding from bulging. Since blank books are made with good paper, you can write down captions, guest lists and other notes to accompany your photographs. Even if you don't keep a book, it's still important to save the pictures: Children will want to see these and relive the party. Years later they may want to use the ideas for their own children's parties.

Classic Party Ideas

HAPPY BIRTHDAY PARTY

Birthday parties are fun for all ages. However, they are not that different from other parties, except for the presents and birthday cake with candles. Many people like to have a theme for a birthday party that corresponds to a season, holi-

day or other event, so you can mix and match the themes for any of the parties: A February birthday could be celebrated with a Valentine party or an October one with a Halloween party.

Almost obligatory at every birthday party is a spirited rendition of "Happy Birthday," sung as the cake is brought forth with the candles burning. The cake can be served alone or as dessert after a light meal, depending on the time of day. For very young children, a meal should be particularly light since their appetites may not be up to a lot of food and excitement at once.

Traditionally the presents are opened right after the cake is served, but this can be varied to suit the occasion. Some parents prefer to separate the two activities; others have gifts first and then the cake. Whether to add family gifts to those brought by other children is a matter of personal preference, but many families save these for a more private party. The birthday child will be getting a lot of gifts as it is, and it is better not to overwhelm a small child or make other children feel left out.

Do be sure to discuss gift-receiving etiquette with your child. He should acknowledge both the gift and the giver as presents are opened. It is also good to remind the child to give each present equal time in the spotlight—and to be careful not to show which he likes best. It may even be necessary to remind a child of this tactfully and privately as gifts are being opened.

Even very young children can understand this etiquette if you say something like, "You know how you would feel if someone didn't pay any attention to the present you gave them." While children sometimes don't seem to care about the

beyond their regular bedtime without disturbing anyone, that's also close enough so that you can be available for nighttime emergencies (and to settle them down if their energy should last *too* long). A movie on the VCR is a good way to settle everyone into their beds, and often puts them to sleep as well. Be sure to have plenty of healthy munchies, such as carrots and celery washed and cut in sticks, unsalted peanuts, popcorn, fruit juices and sandwich meats on hand—raiding the refrigerator is part of the fun!

One advantage to a sleep-over is that the very excitement of a night out and a chance to talk and giggle with friends provides the fun. But you may want to combine this with a few games appropriate to the age group.

Since this is a good party for older children, why not let them make their own dinner or late-night snack by combining it with a pizza party? Or have a sundae buffet with ice cream in several flavors and all the toppings for sundaes and banana splits.

Add a new twist by letting the children make their own pancakes for breakfast. You can make

feelings of others, it is never too early to start teaching social graces. Your children may surprise you with their thoughtfulness, and the party will go much better with happy guests than with children whose feelings have been hurt.

SLUMBER PARTY

Slumber parties are very popular with children, especially girls, but they are more complicated to arrange. Consider where the guests will sleep, what they will sleep in and how they will get home the next day.

Best for children eight or older, sleep-overs are well suited to small groups of close friends. Plan, if possible, to give them their own corner of the house—your child's room, the playroom or a sun porch. Since most children have sleeping bags write, "Bring your own blankets or sleeping bag," on the invitation.

Wherever you have them sleep, it should be a place where they can stay up and talk (or giggle)

several batches of batter and set out bowls of raisins, berries, chopped dried apricots and nuts which each child can add to his or her own bowl of batter. There will be more dishes to wash, but the party will be a memorable event with an upbeat ending.

Make arrangements to get everyone home, and double-check them with parents to be sure no one will be stranded. There won't be a lot of work the morning after; guests usually leave after breakfast. The most confusing part of a slumber party is getting everyone's belongings sorted out!

PARTY OUTINGS

If your home is not large enough for a party or if you would rather have a party somewhere else, there are many possibilities for outings and trips. Cities abound with places, from children's theaters to a children's museum. Some children's museums even offer overnight parties where children can explore the museum after hours, and participate in special programs and projects. And when the time comes, they can unroll their sleeping bags anywhere in the museum that interests them. Museums offer art classes, science explorations and other adventures for small groups. Many even offer a place to serve the cake, or you can have it at a nearby cafe or restaurant.

Even if a museum or aquarium does not have special party programs, a trip there would be a good party in itself. For these trips you should have at least one other adult, even for a few children: A good ratio is one adult for every three small children or every five older children. Many museums have courtyards or lawns that are perfect for picnics, and you can prepare bag lunches or picnic baskets for each guest.

Zoos are always a favorite for children. So are science museums, art museums, wildlife parks and playgrounds.

Courtesy of Texas Highway Department/© Jack Lewis (all)

An outing to a museum of natural history or dinosaur fossil park to learn about dinosaurs makes a great party.

Party Food

Ask anyone, child or adult, what they remember best about a great party, and they're sure to say, "The food." It is the essential ingredient.

If the party is to be held at a regular mealtime, you should serve a full meal. It doesn't need to be elaborate or fancy—hot dogs, grilled hamburgers, pizza and spaghetti are good choices, as are sandwiches. Unless you know the children and their eating habits well, it is best not to stray too far from familiar flavors and dishes. Have your child ask his friends a few days in advance what kinds of foods they like.

Don't serve food that is too gimmicky. Bear in mind that kids eat what tastes good to them, whether it is cute or not. Dressing a hard boiled egg up to look like Humpty Dumpty is not going to get it into the mouth of a child who hates boiled eggs. Flavor is still the most important part of eating. This doesn't mean that all they need is plenty of cake and ice cream, but a party isn't the place to start teaching a varied group of kids about the four food groups.

Since the cake is going to command everyone's attention, you can show off your skills.

THE CAKE

Though cakes are usually associated with birthdays, they often highlight menus for other parties as well. A basic rule is: Kids love cake.

You can choose a plain cake, a cake decorated with fancy designs and writing or one which is sculpted into a fanciful shape, depending on your own ambition or the baker's skill and what your child likes. If your party is for the baby's christening or first birthday, an elegant German or Austrian torte, or a Black Forest cherry cake would be appropriate for the adults who'll make up the guest list. But for young guests, the traditional frosted white or chocolate cake is likely to be more popular.

When you choose a plain round or square cake, the decorative frosting becomes the visual tie-in with the theme. If you are handy with cake decorating, you can create nearly any theme out of frosting. Or you can keep the cake fairly simple

and decorate it with fancy candle holders. You can buy these or make them yourself with oven-hardening modeling clays that come in a variety of bright colors. Clowns, jungle animals, dinosaurs and other figures can carry out your theme and are reusable as well.

Making a cake shaped to fit to your theme is a little more trouble, but it can be half the fun of preparing for the party. Cake pans come in three basic shapes: square, round and tube shaped. Adapt and combine these shapes to form nearly any design. Use frosting to glue pieces together to cover the resulting shape. Using this system you can easily create a snake, a jack-o'-lantern, an igloo or a castle. If your final design has a lot of cut edges, lightly glaze these with a simple mixture of confectioner's sugar and milk. You can easily spread frosting over this glaze after it dries.

Here are the basic recipe for white cake, and instructions for making two different cake shapes. Use these as a starting point.

WHITE CAKE

2¹/₂ cups cake flour, sifted • 2¹/₂ tsp. baking powder • ¹/₂ tsp. salt • ¹/₂ cup butter • 1¹/₄ cup sugar • 1 cup milk • 1 tsp. vanilla • 4 egg whites, stiffly beaten

For best results, have all ingredients at room temperature. Preheat oven to 375°. Butter and flour pan. Combine cake flour with baking powder and salt. In a large bowl, cream butter and sugar. In a separate bowl, combine milk and vanilla. Add this and the flour mixture to the butter mixture alternately, beating after each addition. Gently fold in egg whites. Pour batter into pan. (You may have to double the recipe, depending on the shape of pan you choose). Bake for about 25 minutes, or until a toothpick inserted into the center comes out dry.

SNAKE CAKE

Bake a cake in a circular tube pan or purchase a similarly shaped angel cake at a bakery. Cut the cake in half. Put the two halves on a platter to form an S shape. Cut a 2-inch segment off the tail. Cut this segment into two triangles. Place the two triangles at one end to form a head with open jaws. Attach these pieces with a little frosting. Frost the entire cake in green, then add

splotches of a different shade of green or yellow. Use red candies for eyes and cut a forked tongue from red construction paper.

CHOCOLATE CAKE

1/2 cup vegetable oil • 3/4 tsp. vanilla • 2 ounces chocolate, melted • 2 eggs, well beaten • 2 cups pastry flour • 1 1/2 cups sugar • 2 tsp. baking powder • 1/4 tsp. salt • 1 cup milk

Butter and flour cake pans and set aside. Preheat oven to 350°. Beat together oil, vanilla, chocolate and eggs. In a separate bowl sift together dry ingredients and add to chocolate mixture alternately with milk, beating only enough to blend well. Spread in pans and bake about 30 minutes or until a toothpick inserted in the center comes out clean. Makes two 9-inch circle layers.

CASTLE CAKE

For the castle cake you will need several plain square cakes baked in 8-inch pans, and several small round cakes, 2 or 3 inches in diameter (a cupcake tin is good for these). Frost the tops of the small cakes and stack them to make towers. Frost two of the square cakes and stack them to form the main castle. Place the towers at the corners of the square cake to form your basic castle. Cover it completely with chocolate icing. Score the frosting with a toothpick in a stone pattern.

Create crenels along the top edges using squares of chocolate bars. You can also cut chocolate squares in half to make window slits. You can decorate the turrets with tiny flags on toothpicks, and tiny toy soldiers. This cake is the perfect choice for a fairy tale party, or a medieval theme with knights and dragons.

FROSTING FOR SPREADING

¹/₄ cup butter • ¹/₄ cup milk • Confectioners' sugar

Melt butter and add milk. Beat in enough confectioners' sugar to make frosting thick enough to spread easily. Makes enough to frost one 9-inch layer cake.

DARK CHOCOLATE FROSTING

6 tbsp. softened butter or margarine • ³/₄ cup dark cocoa • 2²/₃ cups confectioners' sugar • ¹/₃ cup milk • 1 tsp. vanilla

In a small mixing bowl, cream softened butter or margarine. Add cocoa and confectioners' sugar alternately with milk. Beat to a spreadable consistency. Add more milk as needed. Blend in vanilla. Makes about 2 cups of frosting.

DECORATOR FROSTING

¹/₂ cup shortening • 1¹/₂ cups confectioners' sugar • 2 tbsp. milk

Cream shortening with confectioners' sugar. Stir in milk. Beat well, adding more sugar as needed to make a stiff enough consistency for use in a pastry bag. Makes enough to frost one 9-inch layer cake.

Classic Party Games

TREASURE HUNTS

These appeal to children of all ages, and can be as simple or as complicated as you like. The easiest treasure hunts involve hiding little prizes all over a room or area in the style of old-fashioned Easter egg hunts. Each child should have a little bag or container. If they have trouble finding things, or if one child seems to be having trouble, you can give hints by saying, "You're getting warm," as they come nearer to a hiding place, and, "You're getting cold," as they move away from the prize.

As you are hiding things, remember the height and reach of the children—the chandelier is not a fair hiding place! The prizes can be pennies, wrapped candy or an assortment of small objects. Balloons and stickers are particularly good prizes.

For preschoolers, hide an assortment of large, colorful wooden beads and give each child a shoelace so he can string a necklace. If one child has found fewer prizes than the rest, set a few aside to hide in easy places right near children who are having trouble hunting. This is a more diplomatic solution than simply handing them the extra beads at the end.

Or you can have the children collect the beads in bags and then give them laces they can string them on. This could be a good activity for the end of the party, while everyone is waiting for their parents to pick them up.

A sticker hunt could end with each child getting a sheet of colored paper to create sticker scenes upon. Duplicate stickers, as well as colored beads, may be traded among the children.

Outdoor parties offer a variety of hiding places, but be sure the clues are secured with thumbtacks, since a breeze could blow them all away! A pirate party could have the treasure in a box decorated to look like a pirate chest, found by reading a map. Use yellow paper and tear the edges to make it look old. Draw the map using landmarks in the yard such as trees, fences and sheds and hedges.

For a circus party, print the messages on balloons as follows: Blow up a balloon and twist the neck without tying it. Write the clue with a felt-tipped pen on the side of the balloon and let the air out of it. The message will become very small. Hide the balloons as clues. The children will have to blow up the balloons to read each clue.

Another balloon treasure hunt is a little more complicated, but good for parties in rooms where it is difficult to hide clues. The clues are rolled up and placed inside balloons, which are then blown up and tied with long strings. The clues can only be retrieved by breaking the balloons. Each clue tells which balloon is next and the balloons are tied in plain sight to objects described in the clues. The trick is to find the balloons in the right order because on the bottom of each clue there is a letter. The children can combine these letters and spell out the location where the treasure is hidden.

If the treasure is hidden in the hall closet, the first clue might say, "the kitchen door—H." In a balloon tied to the knob of the kitchen door could be a clue reading, "the leg of the big green chair—A." Only by finding the clues in the right order will they be able to spell out the hiding place. This game is for children around age eight or older who can read and have the attention span to follow several clues.

Scavenger hunts are good for outdoor parties, especially those with nature themes. They are only appropriate for children who can read, since each child is given a list of things to find. The list will vary with the locale and the season. Such items as a white rock, a leaf that is not green, a seed, something left by man, a piece of wood and something smaller than your little fingernail, can be included on the list. Add items you know are in your yard, and be sure to let everyone know the boundaries so they don't wander too far.

For children who can read, a treasure hunt can take the whole group through a course of messages leading them ultimately to a prize which they will all share or a trove of smaller prizes, each one marked with a name.

The clues should be riddles that require some figuring out. Clues that rhyme are the most fun, but if your gift for verse is limited, any puzzling clue will be just as good. The important thing is the challenge of finding the next clue. A clue hidden inside a cookbook might have the following clue preceding it:

In the room where parents cook,
Inside the cover of a green book,
You'll find a clue on where to look.

Older children might enjoy the double challenge of having to guess the rhyming word to complete the clue. It might read:

In the room where parents cook
You'll find a clue in the green _____.

Some other clues to get you started could include:

Careful! You'll miss it if you blink.
The next clue is on the kitchen _____.

This clue is safe and warm and snug.
It's under a corner of the living room _____.

Before you can gather up your loot,
You must look in the toe of a _____.

Find this one if you are able.
It's under the leg of the kitchen _____.

You'll be nearer your treasure if you're certain,
To look behind the shower _____.

If you like this clue and want one more,
Look behind the closet _____.

If you lift it up and wait for the tone,
You'll find a clue in the _____.

You'll find this clue if you look hard,
Or if you need to measure a _____.
(tape clue to the back of a yardstick)

You'll find treasure, I know you will,
If you look on the window _____.

SPIDERWEBS

If you have a room you can literally tie up for a few hours, have the children play spiderwebs. It's a game that incorporates all the best elements of play and entertainment. Spiderwebs requires skill without being impossible, and cooperation, though it's essentially an individual endeavor. It is noncompetitive, does not involve chance and can be played by all ages. And everyone gets a prize at the end.

The spiderwebs are made up of balls of string or yarn unwound all around a room—around furniture legs, under tables, around sofas. At the end of each string there is a prize.

The best webs are made from balls of yarn—one color for each child—or spools of kite string. It is more difficult if the web is all the same color, so only use plain string for older children. Use different colors for younger guests.

Begin by tying the end of each string to a prize (or to a bag of favors). Hide these prizes, leaving the string visible. Unwind each string all around the room. As you add each new string, intertwine it with the others. Wrap the strings around furniture, around each other—everywhere.

Make the webs simple for younger children and more complex for older guests. Preschoolers will not have the attention span of twelve-year-olds, so use shorter strings for them and don't make the course as complicated. Try to avoid intertwining the strings in such a way that knots will form when they are pulled. When two children's strings meet, they will have to work together to separate them.

If you have a very large room you can substitute crepe paper streamers for string, but they tear easily so the course should be a fairly simple one that involves longer distances but less complicated intertwining.

The prizes at the end of the string can relate to the theme of the party, or can simply be of a general nature.

PIN THE TAIL ON THE . . .

Although the original game is considered by many to be too childish for anyone but preschoolers, it can be made fun for older children with minimal changes in its theme.

The basic game involves posting a large picture of a donkey on a wall and giving each child a paper tail with a circle of tape on the back (tape not only is safer than pins, but it does less damage to the wall behind the picture). Each child in turn is blindfolded, turned around three times and faced in the direction of the donkey. Then the child attaches the tail wherever he or she thinks it belongs, usually to the amusement of the rest of the group. The tails often appear on the nose and other improbable parts of the donkey's anatomy. For older children who have figured out ways to beat the game, try moving the poster after they are blindfolded.

At an Easter party draw a simple rabbit shape and give players cotton balls to pin on the rabbit. For a pizza party, put a large sheet of blank paper on the wall and tape one pizza-sized circle to it for every three players. Give each team three different colored markers and have each person try to divide the pizza into six slices. For a circus party, draw a clown face without a nose and give everyone a small, red balloon to tape where the nose belongs.

GIANT STEPS (MOTHER, MAY I?)

Choose one person to be the leader—perhaps the winner of the previous game might get this position as a prize. Other children line up in a row facing the leader, about fifteen feet, or the length of the room, away. The leader then addresses each child in turn, saying "You may take three (or any number) giant steps." The person called on must say "May I?" to which the leader replies "Yes, you may." The child then takes the designated number of steps, making them as big as possible. Any child who forgets to say "May I?" must return to the starting line and wait for another turn. The leader can also ask for baby steps, leaps and backward steps.

Rotate different children as leaders so that no one assumes too much power. You can vary this game to suit the party theme by calling the leader the clown or the chief, or by calling the steps dinosaur steps or naming them for jungle animals of various sizes.

© Terry Bisbee

SECTION

II

Unique
Children's
Parties

✓ **P**arty **T**heme: South Seas

✓ **O**ccasion: Birthday, pool or beach party

✓ **A**ges: 5 to 12

✓ **I**nvitations: Palm trees and bright flowers

✓ **D**ecorations: Flowers, lanterns, flamingos

✓ **R**efreshments: Luau on the grill

✓ **C**ake: Tropical flower design

✓ **F**avors and **P**rizes: Flower leis, grass skirts, hula hoops

✓ **G**ames and **A**ctivities: Swimming, banana pass, hula hoop contest

✓ **S**pecial **R**equirements: None

South Seas Party

Perfect for a beach or pool party, this theme is also fun in the middle of winter. Everyone should come dressed in his or her tropical best—make sure you state this on the invitation, which should be decorated with palm trees and bright flowers. Seeing everyone reveal bright shorts and sun dresses as they peel off snowsuits and boots is a great way to begin a midwinter party.

Greet arriving guests with paper leis. If the host is a girl, she can wear a grass skirt and—since they are fast and inexpensive to make—give them to everyone as favors, especially if the guest list is short.

If it's a summer party, a luau is the perfect meal. Serve meatballs skewered with pineapple chunks and cooked on a grill. Instead of the kebabs, you could have chicken wings (easy for little hands) grilled over the fire and corn on the cob. Children will enjoy unwrapping the ears of corn to eat them. Tall, iced drinks with a variety of fruit juices would be ideal. Just make sure the chef wears a loud tropical shirt.

The decorations should be big and colorful. For a winter party, cover the room with huge tissue-paper flowers in bright reds, yellows, oranges, pinks and purples. Pin these in clusters on the walls, on furniture and in the windows. Hang paper lanterns if the party is outside, and be sure to have plenty of plastic flamingos on your lawn. You can find these in party supply stores.

To add to the spirit of the party, play a tape or

record of Hawaiian music. Early in the party, give out the favors—hula hoops, of course, will keep things moving.

The cake for a South Seas party is a decorator's dream. Have a baker cover it with bright tropical flower decorations. Or frost it yourself in sea blue, and cover one edge with yellow sprinkles to make a beach. Add palm trees with decorator frosting (see page 33), or buy plastic palm trees at a party store.

A good game for such a carefree party atmosphere is the banana pass. Divide the guests into two teams, mixing heights on each team as much as possible by asking guests to line up by height, then counting off: one, two, one, two, one, two. Line up each team, alternating a tall child with a shorter child, to make the banana pass more difficult. Give the first person in each line a firm, but not green, banana. They must hold them under their chins or between their cheeks and shoulders, then pass them to the next child. No one may touch the banana with his or her hands. The banana is passed from one player to the next until it reaches the end of the line. If anyone drops the banana to the ground or touches it with his or her hands, the team must start passing the banana from the beginning of the line again. The first team to complete one full pass wins.

You can make up your own rules for a hula hoop contest, but it's common simply to see who can keep hula hooping the longest. Depending on the skill of the players, you can award prizes for fancy hula hoop routines as well.

PAPER FLOWERS

1) Cut a sheet of tissue paper in half, lengthwise. 2) Fold one-half into fourths like an accordian, as shown. 3) Round one end with scissors. 4) Unfold it and gather the straight edge to make the center of a flower. Pinch the center and tie it securely with string. Puff the petals to make a showy blossom. Repeat with other pieces of paper. You can make even fuller flowers by using two sheets of petals together.

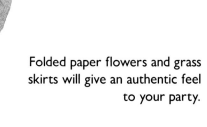

Folded paper flowers and grass skirts will give an authentic feel to your party.

42

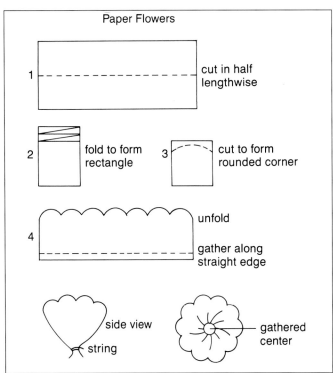

Paper Flowers

1 cut in half lengthwise

2 fold to form rectangle

3 cut to form rounded corner

4 unfold / gather along straight edge

side view / string

gathered center

GRASS SKIRTS

Cut pieces of 1-inch-wide grosgrain ribbon 24 inches longer than the waist measurement of the wearer. Unfold a hank, or coil, of raffia (available at craft supply stores), keeping the strands together. Starting at the top of the hank, using a wide zigzag stitch, sew the raffia to the ribbon. Stitch over it again for reinforcement. Leave 12 inches at each end of the ribbons to tie them.

Measure the raffia to the desired length for the skirt (just above the knee for children) and stitch another length of ribbon to the raffia, without cutting it. Continue to do this until there is not enough raffia for another skirt. Cut the raffia just above each ribbon. Grass skirts are cutest when worn over bathing suits or short-sleeved leotards, accompanied by flower leis.

ROAST CORN IN THE HUSK

Strip back the husks of very fresh ears of corn, but do not pull them off. Remove the silks and soak the ears and husks in a large pot of cold water for 15 minutes. Remove them from the water and bring the husks back to their original position to cover the corn completely. Tie the open ends with string to hold them closed. Roast the ears on the grill for about 20 minutes, or until the corn is cooked. Open an ear to test it before serving the corn to guests.

✔ **P**arty **T**heme: African

✔ **O**ccasion: Birthday

✔ **A**ges: 4 to 12

✔ **I**nvitations: African masks or animals

✔ **D**ecorations: Bright colors, African masks, wild animals

✔ **R**efreshments: Grilled hot dogs, hamburgers or sandwiches

✔ **C**ake: Round cake frosted with zebra stripes

✔ **F**avors and **P**rizes: Miniature carved animals, masks to take home

✔ **G**ames and **A**ctivities: Mask-making, Wari, folk tales

✔ **S**pecial **R**equirements: None

African Party

The African continent is enormously rich in diverse cultures and provides ample possibilities for party decorations and activities.

Its diverse people and animal life offer a wide range of decorations to choose from. You can cover walls with pictures of wild animals cut from brown paper, or with African masks and shields. Striped kikoy cloths from Kenya, or any bright fabric can be used as table coverings or throws for chairs.

Invitations can be constructed in the shape of African masks, or you can use any of the many cards available with wild animals on them.

Favors can include inexpensive wooden animals carved in Kenya, or bright strings of beads. The little carved animals often have loops for hanging and you can put them on narrow ribbons to make necklaces. Animal face masks, which you could make beforehand to give to each child, are available in punch-out books.

Since African food is so different from our own, it would probably be best not to serve it to children. You don't want to have a lot of complaints from finicky eaters. Instead, serve grilled hamburgers, hot dogs, chicken or steak. Many African cuisines use a lot of grilled foods.

Beads are not only popular as jewelry, but they have played an important role in African trade throughout history, so making bead necklaces would be appropriate as well as fun. You can buy beads at hobby stores, or you can get a wide assortment by buying necklaces at thrift shops or flea markets. Nylon fishing line is good thread for stringing. Seat everyone in a circle around small bowls of beads, and let them string necklaces.

Younger children will enjoy a bead treasure hunt (see page 34) or a game of animal charades. Give each child a piece of paper with the name (or picture, for preschoolers) of an animal. The children, in turn, must act out either the appearance or behavior of the animal for others to guess. Pin the Trunk on the Elephant (see page 36) is another possibility for small children.

Masks are an important part of the art and ceremony of many African cultures, and children always enjoy creating masks. Have plenty of brown paper bags on hand, with eye holes already cut. Markers, crayons, feathers, fabric trims and felt scraps are only a few of the decorations that can be used to adorn them. The masks can be as fierce or as pretty as each child's imagination allows.

Nearly all African cultures are rich in folk tales and legends and a good activity involves adding sound effects to these stories. Find a book of African folk tales for children at your local library, and select a story that has several characters or animals in it. Find the characters, animals and other elements of the story that need sound effects, like thunder, wind, rain and drum beats. Assign a noise to each child. Let him or her decide how it should sound. Tell the children to make their assigned noises at the appropriate times in the story.

WARI, TOGOLESE STYLE

This is one of the many ways that Wari is played in Togo, West Africa. You need an egg carton and forty-eight small beans for every two players. You begin by putting four beans in each hole in the egg carton. Then one player chooses a hole and takes all four of the beans out, and drops them one at a time into the next four holes, moving clockwise. When he runs out of beans, he takes the beans from the next hole and starts again. The child keeps doing this until he drops the last bean in his hand into a hole that's followed by an empty one. Then his turn ends. The second player picks up the beans from any hole on his side and starts playing the same way, until he drops his last bean into a hole that's followed by an empty one. The players alternate turns. If at any time after the first round a player adds the fourth bean to a hole, he takes all four beans out of that hole, sets them aside, and continues his turn. The game is over when there are only eight beans left on the board. Those beans go to the last player.

The player with the most beans at the end of the game wins. The strategy involves picking the right hole to start with whenever it is your turn.

African beads and a poster of a monkey are good decorations for an African party.

✓ **P**arty **T**heme: Native American

✓ **O**ccasion: Birthday or Thanksgiving

✓ **A**ges: 4 to 7

✓ **I**nvitations: Birch bark or tepees

✓ **D**ecorations: Big tepees

✓ **R**efreshments: Popcorn, buffalo burgers

✓ **C**ake: Tepee or tom-tom shape

✓ **F**avors and **P**rizes: Tom-toms, headdresses, Native American coloring books

✓ **G**ames and **A**ctivities: Building a totem pole, making tom-toms

✓ **S**pecial **R**equirements: None

Native American Party

Children, especially those in the younger grades, are fascinated by the history of Native American life. This is a natural theme for a party, full of activities and decorative opportunities.

If you live in the north, where birch trees are common, try to find some birch bark from downed wood to write the invitations on. Don't peel it off of live trees. The bark can easily be split into sheets to write on with a ballpoint or felt-tipped pen. Avoid using stereotypical phrases from movies, like "Heap big fun."

If birch bark is not available, cut small tepees out of brightly colored construction paper and write the invitations on them.

Decorate the party with tepees made of lengths of strapping (available at lumber stores) tied at the top and draped with blankets or bedspreads. Or you can wrap the tepees with rolls of brown wrapping paper, beginning at the top and holding the edges together with masking tape. Cut the paper at the bottom and begin near the top again, continuing until the tepee is covered, except for the doorway. Favors can include head-dresses, tom-toms which guests can make for themselves, and coloring books with a Native American theme. Museum gift shops are good sources for party favors.

Be sure to have popcorn and tell the legend some tribes have about why it pops: A little spirit is inside each kernel and as the corn is heated the spirit becomes angry and beats on the kernel so hard that it explodes.

Hamburgers will satisfy the appetites of active children at a Native American party, especially if you call them buffalo burgers. The cake can be decorated to look like a tepee.

Games can include a scavenger or treasure hunt with Native American themes. Try tossing a beanbag through the doorway of the tepee for fun.

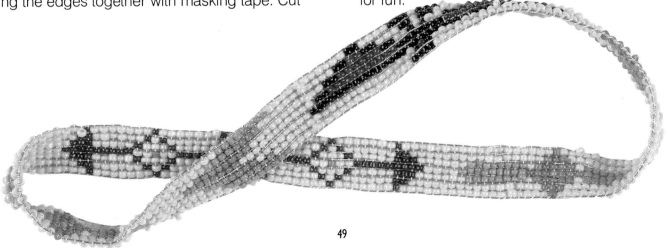

49

TOTEM POLE

Building a totem pole from cardboard cartons is fun for everyone. Have a milk carton or a big cardboard box for each child. Cover the markings on the boxes with white or brown wrapping paper. Give each child markers they can use to draw human or animal faces on the boxes. When the boxes are finished, stack them up to make a totem pole. At the end of the party, each child can take his box home.

A Sioux festival (top); a totem pole from Vancouver, British Columbia.

50

TOM-TOMS

You will need a coffee can (remove the ends with a can opener), two large, strong, round balloons, string and paper for each drum. Cut paper so it will cover the can but not go much beyond the rims. Draw designs on the paper with colored pencils or markers. Then cover the can with the paper and hold it in place at the edges with small pieces of tape. Cut the stem off an uninflated balloon and stretch the rest over the top of the can to make a drumhead. Secure it with an elastic band or by tying string tightly around the top of the can, just under the rim. Leave the bottom of the can uncovered. For the best sound, have the kids hold the drum between their knees and tap it lightly with their fingertips. They should keep their fingers loose, and let them almost bounce off the drum.

FEATHER HEADDRESSES

Measure a length of wide grosgrain ribbon so it is long enough to go around the head of a child with about 3 inches extra. Sew the shafts of long feathers—one or several per band—to the ribbon with a few stitches. Because you fasten these together with safety pins, they can be adjusted to fit any child's head. If you can't find real feathers, you can cut them out of construction paper, but they won't last as long.

TEPEE CAKE

The easiest way to make a tepee cake is to make several round cakes of progressively smaller sizes, just as if you were making layers for a wedding cake. Then angle the edges of each layer by slicing some of the cake off with a knife so that the layers form a tepee shape when stacked. Frost the tepee with a light brown frosting. (See Appendix for information on finding cake pans of graduated sizes.)

✓ **P**arty **T**heme: Dinosaurs

✓ **O**ccasion: Birthday

✓ **A**ges: 3 to 7

✓ **I**nvitations: Dinosaurs

✓ **D**ecorations: Large inflatable prehistoric beasts

✓ **R**efreshments: Simple foods such as slices of pizza, hot dogs or peanut butter sandwiches

✓ **C**ake: Dinosaur

✓ **F**avors and **P**rizes: Stickers, coloring books and small toys in keeping with the prehistoric theme

✓ **G**ames and **A**ctivities: Pin the tail on the tyrannosaurus, spiderweb treasure hunt, dinosaur egg hunt

✓ **S**pecial **R**equirements: None

Dinosaur Party

The prehistoric age of the dinosaur is fascinating to preschool and early school-age children. It is an easy party to decorate, since large dinosaur posters for the walls are easy to find. Dinosaur fabric (available in fabric stores) makes a perfect tablecloth. Inflatable beasts add to the decorations; stand them about the room wearing party hats or holding balloons.

Invitations can be simple dinosaur outlines, or white cards decorated with dinosaur stickers.

Party favors are also easy to find— stickers, small plastic models, barrettes, toys that expand in water and dinosaur coloring books. Look for these small items on the counters of toy stores, children's clothing stores or natural history museums.

Pencils with dinosaur erasers make good prizes for a game of Pin the Tail on the Tyrannosaurus. If you think drawing this beast is beyond your artistic talents, simply cut the tail off a poster of a dinosaur and make photocopies of it at a local copy store. You can color them with crayons before cutting them out. Have the kids pin the tail on the poster.

Start the party with a game of spiderwebs

(see page 36). Food could include hamburgers (call them mammoth burgers) and the cake could take the form of a big, green dinosaur. To settle guests down before eating, have them try their skill at seeing how many words they can make out of the letters in *dinosaur* or, easier, *Tyrannosaurus rex*. Preschoolers could try drawing their own prehistoric beasts with crayons.

Staging a dinosaur egg hunt is similar to staging an Easter egg hunt. Use colorful plastic eggs (buy them at party supply stores). Put coins or small prizes inside them and hide them around the house or yard.

MAKING A DINOSAUR CAKE

A dinosaur can be created from four round cake layers: 1) Cut three of the round layers into ovals by removing crescents from either side.

Each oval should be slightly smaller than the last. 2) Stack these with frosting in between, then trim the top edge of each layer to round the whole shape. 3) Cut one-third off the ends of three of the crescents and frost and stack them to form a tail, as shown. Attach them to the body with frosting. 4) Cut the remaining layer in half, then cut half circles from the center of each half to form two arcs. Cut one third off the end of each arc and use them to make the neck, as shown. Taper the top layer of the neck so it meets the head smoothly. 5) Trim the semicircles and stand them on end to make a head. 6) Glaze the cut edges and frost the entire cake in green. Make "scales" by cutting square tea cookies from corner to corner to form triangles and sticking them upright in the frosting down the length of the back. You can highlight these with frosting along the top edges or leave them plain. Since a cake like this is too large for most cake plates, cover a board or tray with foil and build the cake right on it.

This Segisaurus would be a welcome guest at any child's dinosaur party.

Dinosaur Cake

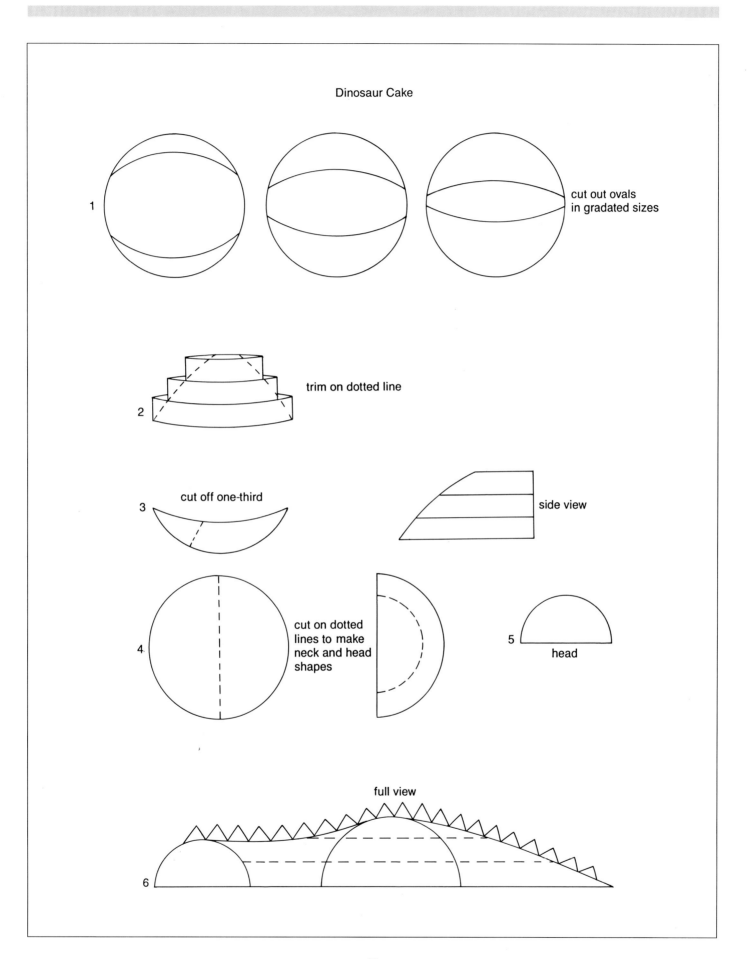

1   cut out ovals in gradated sizes

2   trim on dotted line

3   cut off one-third   side view

4   cut on dotted lines to make neck and head shapes

5   head

6   full view

✓ **Party Theme:** Beach Party

✓ **Occasion:** Birthday or get-together

✓ **Ages:** 5 to 12

✓ **Invitations:** Paper beach balls or pails

✓ **Decorations:** Not necessary

✓ **Refreshments:** Sandwiches, plenty of cold drinks

✓ **Cake:** Stop at an ice cream shop for cake and ice cream

✓ **Favors and Prizes:** Beach toys

✓ **Games and Activities:** Swimming, building sand castles, scavenger hunt

✓ **Special Requirements:** Beach

Party at the Beach

If you live near an ocean or lake, you may want to have a beach party. You'll need plenty of adults to act as lifeguards. Swimming can be the major activity of the day, so you don't have to worry about playing games. Bring plenty of beach toys—beach balls, pails and shovels—or invite the guests to bring their own favorites to share. Give foam kick boards as favors. Be sure to bring along plenty of cold drinks and a bottle of suntan lotion.

Invitations to a beach party can be in the shape of a beach ball, pail, kick board or beach umbrella. Or, make invitations in the shape of watermelon slices.

For these parties, it is best to have a rain date in case the weather doesn't cooperate.

Food is simple: Pack sandwiches and drinks in a cooler or bring a grill for hot dogs. You can return home for the cake and ice cream if it is a birthday party, or you can have them at a local ice cream shop.

A good way to pack lunches for a beach party is to put each one in a new plastic pail, which you give away as a favor. The kids can then use them to save any shells or stones they find.

You can have a beach scavenger hunt for entertainment. A sand castle contest is also fun, and you can be prepared with enough prizes for everyone, rewarding the biggest, the smallest, the most magical, the funniest and the most original. Be sure everyone gets some kind of prize.

SCAVENGER HUNT

Give each child a list of items to find on the beach. The first child back with all the things on the list wins the best prize. You can also give prizes for the most creative finds, or even for the slowest scavenger. Just try to make it so everyone wins a prize of some sort.

Here are some suggested items for the list:

- an animal's home (a *shell*)
- something that was once a rock (*sand*)
- something worn smooth by waves (*beach glass, a stone*)
- examples of three different colors (*shells*)
- something from the land that was changed by the water (*driftwood*)
- something that grows under water (*seaweed or algae*)

✓ **Party Theme:** Pizza

✓ **Occasion:** Birthday or get-together

✓ **Ages:** 6 to 12

✓ **Invitations:** Paper pizza slices

✓ **Decorations:** Red, white and green streamers
(the national colors of Italy)

✓ **Refreshments:** Pizza, of course

✓ **Cake:** A simple cake that's not too rich

✓ **Favors and Prizes:** Small Italian flags, paper chef's hats

✓ **Games and Activities:** Pizza-making

✓ **Special Requirements:** None

Pizza Party

Pizza is most children's favorite party food, so what could be more fun than having them make their own? You couldn't ask for an easier party to plan and give. The main activity and the menu both focus on pizza. Hardly anything can go wrong with pizza as long as you supervise the baking. Unless the children are mature enough to handle hot pans, you should be responsible for putting pizzas in and taking them from the oven. This party is best for small groups of children aged six or older.

Invitations should announce the theme before they are even read, so send a wedge of pizza. Fold a manila folder in half to make it 8¹/₂ inches by 5¹/₂ inches. Cut it into two pieces of 4¹/₄ inches by 5¹/₂ inches. Cut each card into a pizza-shaped wedge, leaving the fold, which will serve as the crust, intact.

Decorate the top of the card with crayons. First draw circles of pepperoni and strips of green pepper, then some yellow cheese. Finally, fill in the background with red for the sauce and highlight the crust with a little brown. Unfold and write the party information on the inside.

MAKING THE PIZZAS

Make the dough ahead of time. A little while before the kids get hungry, have them start making their pizzas. This recipe makes enough for 4 pie-tin pizzas.

PIZZA DOUGH

2 packages dry yeast • Pinch of sugar • 1¹/₄ cups lukewarm water • 3¹/₂ cups white flour • 1 teaspoon salt • ¹/₂ cup olive oil • Inexpensive foil pie tins

Sprinkle dry yeast and sugar into ¹/₄ cup of lukewarm water. Stir lightly and let stand for a few

© Steven Mark Needham/Envision

minutes until mixture becomes bubbly. Sift flour and salt together into a large bowl. Add yeast mixture, stirring well. Keep stirring and add remaining lukewarm water and olive oil. Mix until you can gather the dough into a ball, then turn onto a floured board and knead for about 15 minutes. Set dough in a warm place to rise for about 1¹/₂ hours. Punch dough down and store in a covered bowl in the refrigerator until needed. If you do this more than a few hours in advance, you may have to punch the dough again.

TOPPING

1 to 1¹/₂ cups tomato sauce • 1 to 1¹/₂ cups shredded provolone or mozzarella cheese • Sliced peppers, mushrooms and pepperoni

Preheat oven to 450°. Give each child a pie tin, a lump of dough and table or counter space to work on. Have them pat the dough into a circle to fit the pan, and then add their favorite toppings. If you don't have a big oven, you will have to bake just a few at a time. Bake each pizza for about 10 minutes or until the crust is golden and crisp at the edges. Be sure to warn the children that the pizza is hot.

✓ **P**arty **T**heme: The Olympic Games

✓ **O**ccasion: Birthday or other occasion

✓ **A**ges: 7 to 12

✓ **I**nvitations: Torch design, or card with the Olympic rings on the front

✓ **D**ecorations: None required

✓ **R**efreshments: Hearty, such as hamburgers and hot dogs

✓ **C**ake: Soccer ball or Olympic rings shape

✓ **F**avors and **P**rizes: T-shirts, sports equipment, sweatbands

✓ **G**ames and **A**ctivities: Competitive events

✓ **S**pecial **R**equirements: Field, large yard or gym

Olympics Party

A party of athletics and sports in the spirit of the Olympics is perfect for active children. It's best to hold this party outside, but if you don't have a yard to hold it in, you might consider renting a school, club or YMCA with a gym.

Decorations are unnecessary, except for the table. The centerpiece could be a soccer ball cake. Make a pumpkin cake (see page 79) with white frosting. Mark the soccer ball seams with dark brown decorator frosting, using a pastry bag with a fine tip. Decorate the tabletop with Olympic symbols. Draw soccer balls on heavy paper and use them as placemats. You can buy napkins and plates with sports themes printed on them.

Invitations can be in the shape of a torch, summoning everyone to the Olympic Games. Dress is either sweat suits or gym shorts and tennis shoes, depending on the season.

Prizes will, of course, be medals hung from ribbons striped red, white and blue. Instead of a lot of little favors, have T-shirts printed for the occasion with the five Olympic rings and the date and place of the party. Check with your local sports store to get these. For smaller favors, give sweatbands, jump ropes, Frisbees™, Hackey-Sacks™ or fancy shoelaces.

The main refreshments at the Olympics party shouldn't be served until the last contest is over, but be sure to have plenty of cold drinks and water available at all times. Keep these in official looking coolers and have a stack of hand towels available. You might want to present each guest with a sweatband on arrival.

Be prepared for hearty appetites after the competition. It will be a good time for grilled hot dogs and hamburgers with all the fixings, followed by cake and ice cream in Olympic-sized servings.

OLYMPIC GAMES

Standing Jump: Mark a starting line at one end of a flat piece of ground or on the floor. Have a long tape measure on hand and an official at the starting line. The Olympian stands on the line and jumps forward as far as possible. After the distance is measured and recorded on the score sheet, the next person jumps. Unless there are a great many guests, have each child jump three times. This gives you two ways to score, once for the best average and once for the longest jump.

Running Jump: Use the same system as for the standing jump, but have the Olympian take a running start. His last step must hit the ground behind the starting line. Be sure the athletes have enough room to take a running start of thirty feet.

Foot Races: You will need a stopwatch for this one. If you don't have one, you might be able to borrow one from the physical education department of your child's school. Mark off a starting point and finish line, and have the runners compete one at a time. If you cannot get a stopwatch, have all the runners compete together and use a longer distance so they will finish with enough space between them to be easily judged.

Long Distance Throw: Mark a spot. Have each child throw a softball or beanbag from the spot, and then measure the distance. Again, you can give each child three tries, and score the best average and the longest single throw.

Throw for Accuracy: Hang an old tire by a rope from a tree branch, or stand it on a chair. Have the children throw a softball or beanbag at the hole from a spot six feet away. Give each child three tries. Eliminate those who don't put any shots through the tire, and then move the line back one foot. Continue moving the line back and eliminating players until there is a winner.

Push-ups and Sit-ups: There are two ways to do these in competition. You can judge the Olympians according to endurance by having all the kids do them together on a regular count until all but one drop out. Or you can treat it as a speed event to see who can do the most in thirty seconds. For this you will need to divide the kids into pairs so there is a counter for each Olympian. Then reverse the pairs.

Olympic medals are good rewards for young Olympians; a tug-of-war (left) is always fun; Olympic champion, Jesse Owens (upper left).

OLYMPIC MEDALS

Cut circles about 3 inches in diameter from gold, silver and bronze card stock, available at art or hobby supply stores. Punch a hole in the top of each one and attach a small metal ring (these are called jump rings and are also available at hobby shops). Measure lengths of red-white-and-blue-striped grosgrain ribbon that will fit easily over the head, leaving a few inches for tying the ends together. Run the ribbon through the jump ring and tie it in a small square knot. Be sure you have enough of these to award at the end for such Olympic qualities as good sportsmanship, team spirit or perseverance. Those children who did not win other medals will be happy to get these.

You can award the medals at the end of the Olympics or after each event.

SCORECARDS

Each child will want to remember his or her score, so be sure to provide scorecards. You can make these very inexpensively. Take a sheet of typing paper and fold it in half. Unfold it and write down the name of each sporting event on the right-hand side. Draw two lines under each event that will have multiple scores. Have the sheet photocopied for each guest on vellum paper or light card stock. Then fold each sheet in half so the scoring information is on the inside, on the right. Write each child's name on the front of a scorecard. Decorate them with stickers.

As the games progress, have each child carry his or her card, or keep score yourself on a clipboard. While the children are enjoying their refreshments and well-earned rest, you can transcribe the scores onto the cards.

✓ **Party Theme:** Old-fashioned Independence Day

✓ **Occasion:** Fourth of July

✓ **Ages:** All ages

✓ **Invitations:** Firecrackers

✓ **Decorations:** Red, white and blue

✓ **Refreshments:** Steaks, hamburgers, hot dogs from the grill, corn, watermelon

✓ **Cake:** Red, White and Blue Shortcake

✓ **Favors and Prizes:** Tops, hair ribbons

✓ **Games and Activities:** Colonial games

✓ **Special Requirements:** Yard or other outdoor area

Fourth of July Party

Independence Day is likely to be a hot day, perfect for the beach or anyplace outside. Watermelon, ice cream, strawberry shortcake, grilled hot dogs, steak and corn are good foods for a Fourth of July party.

Decorations should be strictly red, white and blue. Old-fashioned helium balloons and sparklers are traditional. Small flags, streamers and paper plates and cups in red, white and blue will add to the patriotic flair. Party favors can be wooden tops or red, white and blue hair ribbons.

The invitation could have a drawing of a firecracker and say, "You're invited to a bangup Fourth of July." Or you can make the invitation in the shape of a firecracker by rolling colored tissue around a cardboard tube. You could have a cookout and a little party followed by a trip to see the local fireworks display.

Colonial games, such as tops, hoop spinning and hoop rolling will show children how young patriots of two centuries ago celebrated this important day.

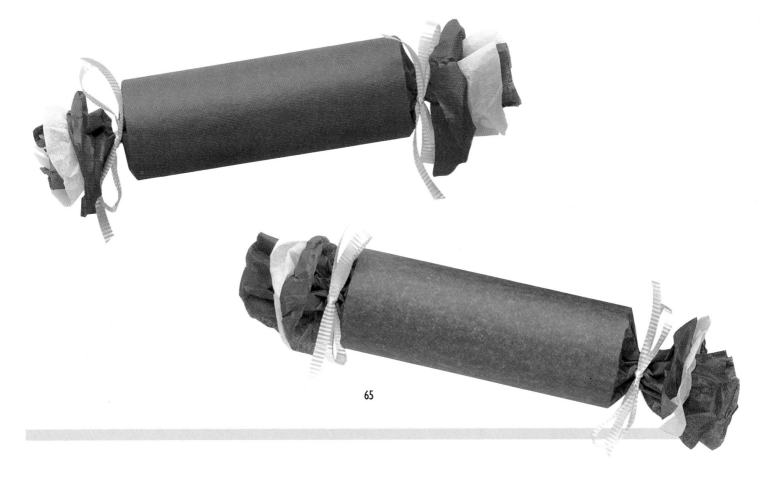

65

RED, WHITE AND BLUE SHORTCAKE

Since holiday parties are likely to be gatherings of adults and children, the activities and foods should appeal to all ages. This seasonal cake is a holiday version of a traditional favorite. Everyone will love it.

2 cups flour • 1/3 cup sugar • 4 tsp. baking powder • 1/2 tsp. salt • 1/4 tsp. nutmeg • 1/2 cup butter • 1 egg • 1/3 cup milk • 1 pint heavy cream • 1 pint blueberries • 1 pint strawberries • Superfine sugar

Generously butter and flour a 9-inch round cake pan and set it aside. Preheat oven to 450°.
Sprinkle one third of blueberries lightly with sugar and set aside. Slice one third of strawberries, sprinkle lightly with sugar and set aside.
In a large bowl, sift together flour, sugar, baking powder, salt and nutmeg. Cut in butter. Combine egg with milk, stirring well, and mix into dry ingredients until well blended. Spread this into the cake pan and bake until nicely browned, about 15 minutes. Split it with forks while it is hot, making two thin layers, and cool them on racks. Whip heavy cream, adding very little sugar. Spread one quarter of this on the bottom layer and cover it generously with sugared blueberries and strawberries. Top it with the second layer and cover the entire cake with the remaining whipped cream. Decorate the top lavishly with remaining blueberries and strawberries.

Hoop rolling: Use hula hoops and 12-inch lengths of 3/4 inch dowel. Stand the hoop up on its edge and start it rolling, then run beside it, keeping it rolling by hitting it with the stick. You can have races if you want.

Hoops and sticks: You can play this with the same dowel and a large wooden embroidery hoop, which can be bought at a needlework shop. Tie several 12-to-13-inch-long red, white and blue streamers or ribbons so they hang in long, flowing strips from the hoop. One player puts the hoop on the stick and throws it to the other player, who tries to catch it on his stick and throw it back.

Horseshoes, tag, hide-and-seek and scavenger hunts work well for this party.

✓ **Party Theme:** Circus

✓ **Occasion:** Birthday

✓ **Ages:** 3 to 12

✓ **Invitations:** Tents or clown faces

✓ **Decorations:** Streamers to form a big top over table, brightly colored balloons

✓ **Refreshments:** Sandwiches

✓ **Cake:** Frosted with a clown's face

✓ **Favors and Prizes:** Balloons, clown makeup, anything with a clown or a circus theme

✓ **Games and Activities:** Elephant piñata, performance by a clown, painting clown faces

✓ **Special Requirements:** None

A One-Ring Circus

Any party with a lot of children has the potential to turn into a three-ring circus, so here are some hints for having a more organized and fun one-ring circus party.

The circus theme offers an endless array of decorating possibilities. No theme beats it for color, excitement, music, costumes or cakes. The party room can be transformed into a big top easily by draping multicolored streamers from the center of the ceiling and taping or tacking them to the surrounding walls at about shoulder height. Gather a bunch of balloons together in the center

© Susanna Pashko/Envision

of the room and give them out as party favors at the end of the party.

Use a bright tablecloth and different colored napkins. This rainbow of colors adds to the general air of excitement and helps kids pretend they are under the big top.

Invitations can be in the shape of tents or clown faces, and you can invite guests to dress as circus performers—clowns, acrobats, lion tamers, ring masters, snake charmers and dancers.

Play Pin the Nose on the Clown, or have a beanbag toss where you aim for the open mouth of a giant cardboard clown face. Party favors are easy to find in stores. Animals and clowns are very popular with young children.

If you want to have a really special party, invite a clown or have someone come over to paint the children's faces. You also could paint the children yourself, using the clown makeup sold at toy stores.

ELEPHANT PIÑATA

Smashing the piñata is one of the most popular party games of all time. It's a game with laughter, suspense, action and prizes for everyone.

It's not too hard to make an elephant piñata for your circus party. And you and your child will have fun doing it. All you need is a large balloon, plenty of newspaper, colored tissue paper, construction paper, heavy twine, flour and water, small gifts and candy.

First, blow up the balloon and tie it shut. This balloon will form the body of the piñata. (In the end, the balloon will be popped and the cavity will be filled with prizes.) Mix flour and water to the consistency of paste: It should be thick, but runny enough to seek its own level when stirred. Tear some newspaper into strips no more than 1 inch wide. Dip the strips into paste one at a time and lay them across the balloon. Continue tearing newspaper strips and gluing them to the balloon until it is completely covered.

Wrap the twine once around the balloon and tie it at the top with enough loose twine hanging from the knot to make a loop to hang the elephant by. Then continue to wrap the balloon with newspaper strips until they are several layers thick. If the balloon is dripping with glue, use one layer of dry newspaper strips at the end.

Hang the piñata and allow it to dry thoroughly. This may take two or three days in humid weather. When the papier-mâché is hard, cut a 2-inch hole with a sharp knife at the top near the hanging loop; remove that section of the shell and save it. The balloon will break when you do this. Hang the piñata shell again so it dries thoroughly on the side.

Once the basic shell is dry, you can begin to add the other features—neck, head, legs, trunk, whatever else is needed to give you the shape of an elephant. Use rolls of newspaper held together with tape (keep them hollow to cut down on weight) for the legs and trunk. Attach them to the body with masking tape and then blend them in with a thin layer of papier-mâché. (Foam cups, cardboard tissue-paper rolls and crumpled newspaper can also serve as the base for legs, trunks and ears.) Cover all these with just enough papier-mâché to hold the shape, since this portion is for decoration only and will not have to hold any prizes. Allow them to dry thoroughly. By now the shape should look pretty much as it will remain.

Now you are ready to cover the piñata with a tissue paper skin. Choose a color of tissue for the skin and cut it in 2-inch-wide strips. Fold these in half lengthwise and score the folded edge with

© Tony Cenicola

3/4-inch slashes, cut about 1/4 inch apart. Cover the entire elephant with these strips, wrapping them in loops around the elephant, beginning at one end. Glue the cut edges down and leave the scored edge free. The scored edge of each layer should hide the glued edge of the previous row and make the piñata frilly. Don't cover the hole.

Let the tissue paper skin dry. Then fill the piñata with lots of little party favors and candy through the hole. Finally, fit the piece you saved back in the hole and seal it with papier-mâché or tape. Cover this with more colored tissue paper. Then hang the piñata.

When the time comes to break the piñata, have all the kids gather together in a circle around it. Make sure the kids are several yards away from the piñata. Then blindfold the birthday child with a bandana. Put a plastic bat in the child's hands, and spin him around gently two or three times. Tell him to try to hit the piñata with the bat. Give him a few swings, then switch to another child, continuing until the piñata breaks. This game requires close supervision so none of the guests are struck. As soon as the piñata bursts, take the blindfold off and let all the kids gather as many prizes as they can.

Party **T**heme: Autumn leaf collecting

Occasion: Birthday or get-together

Ages: 5 to 12

Invitations: Brightly colored paper leaves

Decorations: None, unless the group is returning home for refreshments, in which case you can decorate with leaves, pumpkins and a general fall motif

Refreshments: Sandwiches, cider, apples, trail mix

Cake: No cake necessary

Favors and **P**rizes: Spatter prints to take home

Games and **A**ctivities: Gathering leaves, scavenger hunts, outdoor games and spatter painting

Special **R**equirements: Plenty of trees

Autumn Celebration

If you live in an area where the leaves turn rich, vibrant colors in the fall, a leaf-collecting excursion is a nice group activity for an autumn afternoon. It is a low-key party which you can have at a public park if you don't have woodlands near your home.

Invitations can be written on bright leaf shapes cut from construction paper. They should remind guests to wear outdoor play-clothes and sturdy shoes for walking.

You will need extra adults at the party to help keep track of everyone. Hand out bags (these can be drawstring bags made of autumn-colored fabric, or just plain paper or plastic bags) and have the children collect the prettiest leaves they can find. Take along a small nature guidebook to help answer the inevitable question: What kind of leaf is it? See how many different leaf varieties and colors each child can find. This is a perfect opportunity for children to learn a little about the natural world while having fun.

If you plan to picnic outside, take along fresh cider and sandwiches. Crisp red apples and ginger cookies are also good for autumn picnics. Or you can give each child a package of trail mix to munch on and then serve refreshments when you return home. Be sure everyone collects their trash before you leave.

Scavenger hunts, tag and hide-and-seek are good games to play if the entire party is to be outdoors.

If you are going indoors after the leaf walk, you can help the guests put the brightest and prettiest leaves between sheets of waxed paper to preserve them. Go over the leaves gently with an iron set on low. Cut the waxed paper in circles around the leaves, tape a piece of string on the back and tell the children to hang them in their windows at home to catch the sun's rays.

LEAF SPATTER PRINTS

Each child will need plain heavy paper, watercolors or tempera paint (you can have several children share large jars of paints or put several portions into small jars or lids), an old toothbrush and a stick, which they can find on the walk. Cover the work area well with newspaper. This is a good project to do in the middle of the floor.

To make a print, place a leaf on the plain paper. If you're using watercolors, wet the toothbrush and rub it in the paint. If you're using tempera, tip the jar to get a light layer of paint on the edge, then rub the brush in it to coat the ends of the bristles lightly. Holding the brush, bristles down, about twelve inches above the paper, make a fine spray of paint by rubbing the brush back and forth over the stick so the paint splatters over the leaf. The covered area will remain unpainted, leaving the perfect shape of the leaf.

Suggest that the children experiment, using several leaves or colors in a design. They may want to use slightly heavier paper cut into squares and make the designs into greeting cards, or decorate large sheets for wrapping paper. Be sure to put each child's initials on the prints before setting them out to dry.

TRAIL MIX

This delicious, healthy blend of nuts and dried fruits is easy to make, carry and eat. It can be as plain or complicated as you like. Mix together unsalted peanuts (usually well-liked even by children who don't like other nuts), raisins, chopped dried apricots, pumpkin seeds, almonds and whatever other dried ingredients you like. A good place to look for these is in the bulk-food bins of a grocery store or natural foods shop. Divide the mix into bags to be passed out.

✓ **Party Theme:** Scary!

✓ **Occasion:** Halloween

✓ **Ages:** All ages

✓ **Invitations:** Haunted house or coffin

✓ **Decorations:** Bats, pumpkins, spiderwebs, dim lights

✓ **Refreshments:** Easy-to-eat foods

✓ **Cake:** Pumpkin

✓ **Favors and Prizes:** Fabric trick-or-treat bags, masks

✓ **Games and Activities:** Treasure hunt by flashlight, spiderwebs, mask-making, fortune-telling

✓ **Special Requirements:** A room that can be darkened is fun, but not essential

Halloween Party

More and more parents are giving Halloween parties as an alternative to trick-or-treating. They're more safe, and can even be more fun.

Invitations to Halloween parties can have as many themes and motifs as cakes do. Jack-o'-lanterns, black cats, ghosts and bats are all good shapes. A black haunted house could be opened to reveal a white ghost on which the invitation is written. Or a black coffin could open to show a mummy. Halloween stickers provide a good way to decorate invitations, too.

The very wording of the invitation can foretell the spooky experience ahead. The place might be given as "The haunted house at 36 Main Street"; the host's name might be "The Wicked Witch, Sally" or "Pete, the Pirate"; you could write, "Beware of vampires in the yard," or "Mummies welcome" at the bottom of the card. Costumes are, of course, obligatory—and the more outrageous the better. For older children you can specify that the costume must be made or assembled by the child, which gives rise to original getups for gypsies, pirates, space aliens, kings and queens.

An alternative is to have costume materials on hand and let everyone make their costume right there. Have magazine pictures available for kids who need help with their ideas. Construction paper, paper bags, aluminum foil, sheets, old curtains, hats, jewelry, crepe paper and tissue paper are among the items you should have on hand. This is more suitable for older children who can use scissors safely. Prizes can be awarded in enough categories, like the funniest, most elegant, prettiest, silliest and most unusual, so that everyone wins something.

Decorating for a Halloween party is a family project that everyone will enjoy. Black paper streamers, construction-paper bats hung from threads, dim lights (or no lights at all), evil-faced jack-o'-lanterns with flashlights inside and scary noises playing on the tape recorder (you can make your own or buy ready-made tapes) all add to the spooky atmosphere.

77

The possibilities are endless. If you darken the room almost completely, you can make a haunted house, a cave or a dungeon. Hang long pieces of string and fiberfill cobwebs from the ceiling. Make a coffin from cardboard cartons painted black. The coffin lid can even open mysteriously at some point (pulled by a hidden black string). An older sister or brother can dress as Dracula or a mummy and welcome arriving guests. Ask each child to bring a flashlight if the room will be dim. Hang cobwebs and bats the height of the children's faces.

Mask making is a perfect activity. Provide plain half masks (the kind used for New Year's masquerades) and an assortment of feathers, sequins, glitter, crepe paper, yarn for hair and construction paper. Paper plates with the eye holes already cut out are good mask bases, too.

Older children may enjoy creating their own monster faces with papier-mâché and facial tissues. Using cotton cosmetic puffs, cover the face with the papier-mâché mixture and strips of facial tissue. Leave area around eyes, nostrils and lips uncovered. Work with one area at a time until face is covered with tissue. Then apply the colored paste over the white areas as desired. You can build up several layers to change the shape of the face or create warts or horns. You will need plenty of mirrors for this, so give inexpensive hand mirrors as party favors.

Fortune-telling is a good activity for a Halloween party. You will need someone to dress up as a gypsy, with a long skirt, shawl and scarf. A round rose bowl (from the florist) or fishbowl makes a good crystal ball. Line the bowl loosely with light green tissue and place a small flashlight inside to give it an eerie glow. The gypsy can make up outrageous good fortunes.

Children love costumes (opposite page); Lon Chaney, Jr. was the ultimate Frankenstein.

© Movie Still Archives

FACE PAPIER-MÂCHÉ

6 tbsp. cornstarch • 2 tbsp. flour • ½ cup white corn syrup • ½ cup water • Red, green and blue food coloring.

In a bowl, mix cornstarch with flour. Add corn syrup and water, and stir until smooth. Divide half the mixture among three small bowls, and leave half in the original bowl. Add red, green and blue food coloring separately to the small bowls. To use, dab the mixture on one area of the face at a time, avoiding the eyes, and cover it with strips of facial tissue. To remove, gently peel the papier-mâché off. Wash the face carefully with soapy water to remove the papier-mâché.

GREEN GOO PUNCH

1 quart-size envelope instant lemonade mix, prepared according to package directions • 1 quart grapefruit juice • 1 liter lemon-lime soda • Green food coloring, optional

In a large bowl, combine lemonade, grapefruit juice and soda. Add a little green food coloring, if desired. Serve from a deep pot or a bowl covered with black tissue to look like a cauldron.

PUMPKIN CAKE

A pumpkin cake is assembled from a single round cake layer and two more spherical cakes baked in oven-proof mixing bowls. The batter is the standard white-cake recipe. Be sure to grease the bowls well. Don't overfill them, or the cakes won't rise properly. Bake them according to the standard white-cake recipe. Then cool them and stack them with a mixing bowl layer, round side down, on the bottom, followed by the regular layer, and finally the other mixing bowl layer, so that the cake looks like a pumpkin. Frost it with orange icing. Push a ladyfinger or an oblong cookie into the top for a stem and cover it with green decorator icing (see page 33). Paint a jack-o'-lantern face on one side with chocolate decorator icing.

✓ **P**arty **T**heme: Dressing up

✓ **O**ccasion: Birthday

✓ **A**ges: 3 to 12

✓ **I**nvitations: Plumed hat

✓ **D**ecorations: The outlandish costumes will be enough

✓ **R**efreshments: Easy-to-eat sandwiches, such as peanut butter, ham or cheese, cut into triangles

✓ **C**ake: Fancy

✓ **F**avors and **P**rizes: Feathers, outrageous jewelry from the thrift shop, scarves

✓ **G**ames and **A**ctivities: Dressing up, guess who, charades

✓ **S**pecial **R**equirements: Materials to make costumes

Elegant Costume Party

Particularly suited to girls of any age, dress-up parties are also popular with younger boys. Your first stop in preparing for this party is the thrift shop—unless, of course, your children are so fortunate as to have a grandmother, aunt or neighbor who keeps a costume trunk. An alternative is to borrow the costumes from a school where they are kept for plays. You will need at least a few dresses, skirts and slacks. You can add scarves, shawls, hats and accessories from your own collection (not things you value). Sheets, old drapes and curtains make fine robes, trains and togas. You can also vary the assortment by inviting the children to bring any favorite costumes or dress-up clothing they may have. Search your bureau for old gloves and jewelry.

Depending on the age of the children, and how their parents feel, you can provide makeup, such as rouge and eyebrow pencil, to heighten the effect of the glamorous costumes.

For children who can read, you might go to the library and find a book of simple plays. Choose one involving kings and queens or other fancifully dressed characters. You can draw lots for characters or choose them ahead of time and have the children bring some of their own costumes. Copy the play so that everyone has a script.

Invitations to the dress-up party can be cut in the shape of hats and decorated with plumes, which are available at hobby and craft shops.

Games for this party might include Guess Who, in which each player imitates a famous person or character whose name has been drawn from a hat. Good names include the Queen of Hearts, King Arthur, Robin Hood, Dorothy and the Wicked Witch of the West from *The Wizard of Oz* and other names from stories or movies your children know. Be sure to provide construction paper, scissors and tape for making crowns and other props.

Since the costumes will probably be elegant and flowing, with floppy sleeves, it is best to keep foods simple and easy to eat. But this doesn't mean the food can't be elegantly presented. Cut sandwiches in fancy tea shapes, and serve little skewers of cubed meat and cheese.

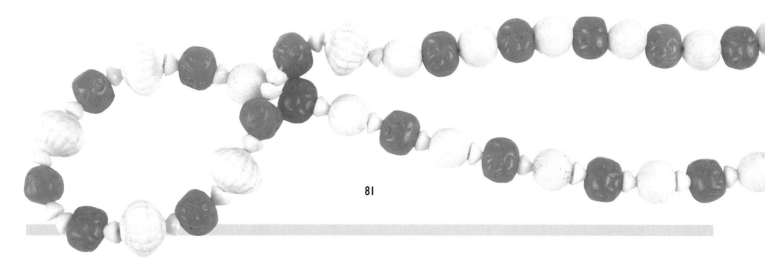

82

MAKING COSTUMES FROM SHEETS, CURTAINS AND SCARVES

■ **Sarong:** Wrap a large piece of fabric around the child's waist to form a skirt, then bring the loose end up and tuck it into the waistband.

■ **Gypsy skirt:** Tuck several large square scarves into a belt, tucking about one quarter of their length under with the points facing down. For a gypsy belt, fold a square scarf diagonally. Tie it around the waist with pointed end down over one hip and the knot over the other.

■ **Toga:** Wrap one end of a folded sheet around the waist, and tuck it into a belt. Bring the free end up over one shoulder and let it hang down.

■ **Bridal veil:** Tuck a lace curtain or a sheer scarf into a headband and let it trail behind.

■ **Princess hat:** Make a hat by rolling a large piece of paper into a cone, and attach the ends of a sheer scarf to the tip and the base, letting it drift behind.

■ **Turban:** Wrap a long narrow scarf around the head, tucking the tails inside just behind the ears.

■ **Shawl:** Tie a square scarf in half (so that it forms a triangle) and drape it over the shoulders.

■ **Babushka:** Tie a square scarf, folded in half, under the chin, pulling it slightly over the face.

■ **Pirate:** Fold a square scarf diagonally, and then into a wide band. Tie it around the forehead, pulling it down to cover one eye.

Your guests will love to dress up with lace and costume jewelry.

✓ **P**arty **T**heme: Winter sports

✓ **O**ccasion: Birthday or get-together

✓ **A**ges: 4 to 12

✓ **I**nvitations: Mittens

✓ **D**ecorations: None required

✓ **R**efreshments: Hot chocolate and hearty, warm foods, like chili

✓ **C**ake: Igloo cake

✓ **F**avors and **P**rizes: None

✓ **G**ames and **A**ctivities: Skating or sledding

✓ **S**pecial **R**equirements: Snow-covered hill or skating rink

Winter Fun

Winter weather gives you the theme and activities for a great party. If you live near a good hill or a skating rink or pond (make sure the ice is safe), you can have a winter party close to your home.

Cut out invitations in the shape of a mitten. Invitations are very important for this party, since they let the guests know that they should wear warm clothes and bring skates and sleds. If the guests will be coming to your home, the invitations might also suggest that the kids bring dry socks and pants to keep them warm after they come inside.

Greet everyone with hot chocolate from a thermos when they arrive at the pond or hill. And if you want, give everyone a hearty meal of chili, macaroni and cheese or thick soup after the activities. If it's a birthday party, the cake can follow any theme appropriate to the children's ages, or you can have an igloo cake. Bake it as directed for the pumpkin cake (see page 79), but leave off the bottom round layer. Frost it with white icing and mark the lines of snow bricks with decorator frosting colored with black food coloring (see page 33). A small entryway for the igloo can be made from a piece of extra cake.

You don't need to organize games and activities, but you should plan to have other adults there to help everyone tie their skate laces and fix obstinate jacket zippers. Younger children will need supervision on the ice and on the hill. You might want to bring spare mittens to replace lost or wet ones.

The length of the party will depend on the ages of the children and the temperature. The younger the children and the colder the weather, the shorter the party.

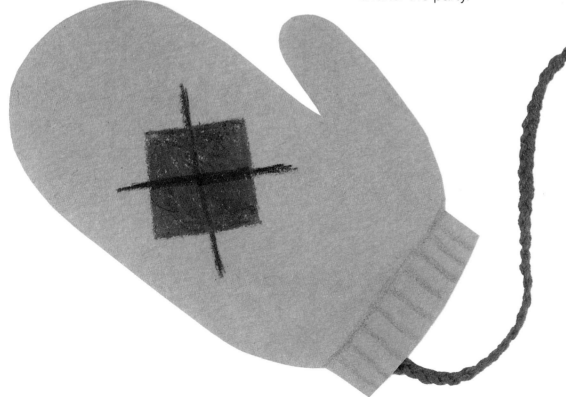

ICE CREAM
IN THE SNOW

Even children whose families make ice cream at home will be amazed by this simple method for making their own ice cream. Each child will need an empty can. Soft drink cans without their tops work best, but other cans about the same size will do. If the edge is sharp, cover it with masking tape. Each child will also need a plastic container. Cut off the bottom half of a gallon milk jug for this.

Sprinkle a little rock salt in the bottom of the plastic jug and put the can inside it. (It doesn't matter if the can is a little taller than the plastic container.) Pack about 1 inch of clean, untrampled snow into the plastic dish around the can, sprinkle with a little more salt and continue making layers until the plastic dish is full. In each can pour about ½ cup of milk, 2 tablespoons of evaporated milk and 2 teaspoons of sugar. Add about 1 teaspoon of chocolate syrup.

Give each child a table knife and show them how to stir slowly and evenly, scraping the ice that forms on the inside of the can into the center so that more of the mixture can freeze. In about 15 minutes, the mixtures will be like a thick milkshake and ready to eat. By this time the cans will only be half as full as when they started. This isn't based on any scientific principle, but on the nature of children, who will sample the ice cream often to see if it is ready yet!

Paper mittens (this page) make great invitations to a winter sledding party (opposite page).

✓ **Party Theme:** Swiss mountain life

✓ **Occasion:** Birthday or get-together

✓ **Ages:** 6 to 10

✓ **Invitations:** Paper mountains

✓ **Decorations:** Posters of Switzerland

✓ **Refreshments:** Cheese melts

✓ **Cake:** Chocolate fondue instead of cake

✓ **Favors and Prizes:** Miniature Swiss chocolates, embroidered hair bands

✓ **Games and Activities:** Heidi of the Alps, treasure hunt

✓ **Special Requirements:** None

An Alpine Party

Most youngsters are familiar with the story of Heidi and her lovely homeland in the Alps. This tale is a good backdrop for a wonderful party, especially for younger children. You can easily cover your walls with tall, pointed mountains cut from rolls of paper. Decorate the center of the table with a wide embroidered cloth and hang cowbells from the ceiling if you can find them. Use bright paper plates and cups in primary colors, and choose a red-and-white checked cloth or other bright print for the table.

The story of Heidi, complete with songs, is available on records. Play it as children are arriving. Or have someone read the book out loud. You can make a mountain-shaped invitation from white art paper. Color the lower slopes green and leave the summit white.

Favors could be hair bands made of narrow embroidered trim, or miniature bars of Swiss chocolate. You could play Pin the Tail on the Goat, or Pin the Bell on the Cow.

Cheese melts are a popular alpine food and are easy to prepare. Broil slices of bread—good, firm bakery bread is best—just long enough to toast them slightly. Then cover them with slices of cheese. Choose types that are popular with children, such as mozzarella, very mild Cheddar or American cheese. Put the bread slices back under the broiler until the cheese is just melted and serve them with glasses of ice-cold milk and crisp apple wedges.

The hit of the party will be another Swiss dish, chocolate fondue. It can be a bit messy, but everyone will love it. Tie large napkins around each guest's neck to keep clothes clean. Even if this is a birthday party, this dessert is so special that you will want to forgo the traditional cake—or perhaps just serve each guest a small cupcake.

The Swiss Alps provide a dramatic backdrop for a party inspired by Heidi.

CHOCOLATE FONDUE

2 12-ounce packages semisweet chocolate chips • 1 pint strawberries • 2 bananas • 1 peach • 1 apple • 1 can pineapple chunks • 3 kiwi fruits • 2 tangerines

In the top of a double boiler, over hot but not boiling water, melt the chocolate chips. Wash and hull the strawberries, slice the bananas thickly, peel and slice the peach, cut the unpeeled apple in chunks, drain the pineapple chunks, peel and slice the kiwis thickly and divide the tangerines into segments. Fruits that are juicy or have been washed, such as strawberries, should be dried on paper towels.

Place the chocolate, which should be melted but not hot enough to burn the tongue, in a dish at the center of the table. Each child spears the fruit with a fork, swirls it quickly in the chocolate, and holds it a moment over a plate to cool it slightly before eating it. Have a second batch of chocolate ready, because as the first one cools it will thicken and the coatings will become very heavy. When this happens, replace it with a fresh batch, and reheat the old batch. Do not put chocolate directly over the heat or on an open flame. Each batch serves four or five children.

✓ **P**arty **T**heme: Gingerbread children, "gingerbread" houses

✓ **O**ccasion: A winter party

✓ **A**ges: 5 to 12

✓ **I**nvitations: Paper gingerbread children, houses

✓ **D**ecorations: Gingerbread children and Christmas motif

✓ **R**efreshments: Simple sandwiches

✓ **C**ake: Gingerbread

✓ **F**avors and **P**rizes: Finished cookies and "gingerbread" houses to take home

✓ **G**ames and **A**ctivities: Making cookies and houses

✓ **S**pecial **R**equirements: An oven and table space

Gingerbread Party

The spicy fragrance of gingerbread in the oven is so heady that it can make you want to invite everyone over for a party. You should serve it without fear, because gingerbread is one of the easiest baked goods to make. Give a box of gingerbread people as party favors.

The invitations can easily be cut from brown construction paper or even a smoothly ironed brown grocery bag (which is easier to write on) in the shape of a gingerbread boy, girl or house. Allow plenty of time for this party, since small children will work slowly and older children will get caught up in the fun and want to make more and more.

This is one party that should *begin* with refreshments, since the gingerbread ingredients are so tempting that the children might fill themselves up while they are cooking. If they have just eaten, guests are less likely to eat large quantities of raw dough.

Placecards can be created from gingerbread. Make a cake in a gingerbread man cake tin, and frost it. Decorate the table with gingerbread people, or if you are ambitious, make a gingerbread house for a centerpiece. After refreshments, clear the table for workspace, or move to another large table where everyone will have plenty of elbow room.

Have several batches of modeling gingerbread dough on hand. Although it is designed for modeling stiff cookies that hold their shape when baked, it can also be rolled flat for gingerbread people made with cookie cutters. Younger children might have an easier time with these. Be sure you have enough cutters to go around, preferably in a variety of shapes and sizes.

Along with the decorations for the cookies, such as currants and raisins for eyes, and buttons, or silver shot and colored sugars, you should have a variety of tools including table knives, toothpicks and forks, to use in shaping the dough. Each child should have a large piece of waxed paper to work on.

As the cookies are completed, place them on sheets, which you can place into the oven as each is filled. If you expect problems claiming cookies afterward, simply make a map of the cookies before you bake them. Just write the child's name and the general location of his cookies on a piece of paper. Take them off the sheet in the same order, then slip the sheet under the cooling rack. You will need several cookie sheets and several cake racks for this party.

MODELING
GINGERBREAD DOUGH

4 tbsp. sugar • ½ cup molasses • 2 tbsp. vegetable oil • 2 tbsp. milk • 2⅓ cups flour • ½ tsp. baking soda • ½ tsp. salt • 1 tsp. cinnamon • ½ tsp. ginger

Preheat oven to 350°. Mix sugar with liquids and stir well. Reserve ¼ cup of flour, sift together dry ingredients. Combine these with liquids, in four additions, mixing well. Work the dough with your hands until it is smooth. If it seems too soft for modeling, add a little more flour; if it is too crumbly, add a few drops more milk. The dough will easily form a neat ball when it is the right consistency.

To model people, begin with two balls, a larger one for the body and a smaller one for the head. Flatten them with your thumb or the bottom of a glass dusted with flour. Then add arms and legs, clothing, hats, scarves—whatever details you like. Have pictures on hand to give your young artists some ideas. Remind them that their gingerbread boys and girls need gingerbread cats and dogs, as well as teddy bears.

Bake the modeled figures about 10 minutes. Let them cool just a few minutes on the cookie sheet before removing them to racks. If these are to be used just as decorations, push metal hooks into them just as they come out of the oven; then allow the cookies to dry out and become hard.

Be sure to tell your guests to store their cooled cookies in a tight tin or plastic box when they get home so they will stay soft and chewy.

GINGERBREAD HOUSES

The basic ingredients for these houses could not be simpler. Just use graham crackers and royal icing (and food colors to color the icing if you want). Most gingerbread houses use only white icing since it looks like snow and icicles on the house, but you may wish to use a variety of colors. When you are working with the icing, put a small amount out in a plastic dish and keep the rest tightly covered, since it dries out quickly.

Each house requires eight graham-cracker squares, but you will want to have plenty of extras in case any break. Use a sharp knife to separate the crackers along the scored line so they break evenly.

Lay one cracker flat near the center of the cardboard or pie-tin base. Spread frosting along two opposite outer edges and stand a cracker at each end, outside the base cracker, so that their edges are sitting on the cardboard. Hold them upright for a couple of minutes until the frosting sets. Be sure they are straight.

Spread frosting on three outer edges of another cracker and carefully place it *inside* the two standing walls, with its bottom on top of the cardboard base. It should fit just inside the two end walls, and stand a tiny bit higher. Allow 1 or 2 minutes for this frosting to set, while you repeat this with the fourth wall. Your house should now be able to stand up by itself.

Cut a cracker diagonally into two triangles with a very sharp knife, first perforating it in a straight line. Do this yourself, perhaps before the party, since it is tricky to keep the cookies from breaking. If they are very brittle, hold them one at a time, with tongs (so you don't scald your hand), over the steam from a pan of boiling water to soften them slightly before cutting.

Spread frosting along the base (cut) edge and carefully stand the triangle on the top of one end wall. Hold this in place until it is dry. Repeat this with the other triangle. Frost three edges of each roof piece and lay in place over the top of the house.

Longer houses can be made by leaving the graham crackers in pairs, using split ones only for the ends.

Wait about 20 minutes before decorating the house. This is a good time for the children to stretch and play a while, before they get to the serious business of decorating their houses.

Before the kids begin decorating, suggest some ways they might use the various materials you have on hand. Show them how to frost the roof and then lay rows of slate, beginning at the bottom edge and overlapping each row slightly. Or they may wish to simply cover the roof with snow and add a piece of candy cane for a chimney.

Older children may want to add graham-cracker chimneys or entryways, or even front porches with candy-stick pillars. Licorice laces, clipped into short lengths with scissors, are perfect for outlining windows and doors. Gumdrops or peppermint drops make a pretty decoration along the ridge pole, and the rounded tops of

candy canes make splendid fan windows over front doors.

When the house is finished, spread a light coating of frosting snow around the base and make a front walk from Necco Wafers™ or flat mints. You can landscape the yard with trees made of spearmint candy leaves or large marsh-mallows, which look like snow-covered shrub-bery. A candy cane lamppost might add just the right touch for the front yard.

ROYAL ICING

3 egg whites • 1-pound package confectioners' sugar, sifted • 1 tsp. vanilla • ¹⁄₂ tsp. cream of tartar

In a mixing bowl, combine all ingredients and beat with an electric mixer until frosting is very stiff. This may take 7 to 10 minutes. Since you don't want the frosting to dry out before you use it, keep it covered with a damp kitchen towel.

Makes 3 cups.

Party **T**heme: Tea Party

Occasion: Valentine's Day

Ages: 7 to 12

Invitations: Very elegant with hearts and flowers, woven heart basket

Decorations: Hearts and flowers, lace

Refreshments: Tea sandwiches, Russian tea, fancy cookies and tarts

Cake: Valentine cake

Favors and **P**rizes: Woven heart baskets, with valentine stickers or hair ribbons

Games and **A**ctivities: Parlor games, such as charades

Special **R**equirements: None

Valentine's Day Party

No other holiday has easier decorations. Anyone can draw or cut out a heart and decorate it to make a valentine. The occasion is perfect for a lacy and elegant tea party.

The invitations should be hearts. You can make the card itself a heart, or glue one to the front of a plain card. Perhaps the fanciest of all would be a woven Scandinavian heart basket made of paper, with the invitation tucked inside it. (To be technical, the straight-sided heart created by this basket is not used for Valentine's Day in Scandinavia; it is the Christmas heart, and the valentine heart has rounded sides. But that is a fact that only your Danish friends would notice.)

If you choose a tea party, you will want to serve Russian tea (see page 107), a combination of tea and fruit juices that is a great favorite of children. Tea sandwiches, which can be cut with heart-shaped cookie cutters, can be followed by dainty sugar cookies frosted in pink and decorated with red sugar sprinkles, silver shot, cinnamon hearts or valentine candies.

The dress and setting are, of course, quite formal. This is definitely not a party for toddlers. It is for young ladies and gentlemen on their very best behavior. The tea should not last too long. You might follow it with an old-fashioned parlor game like charades.

If you choose a simpler invitation, the woven heart baskets would make lovely table favors. Fill them with an assortment of stickers to use on valentines, or a few satin hair ribbons.

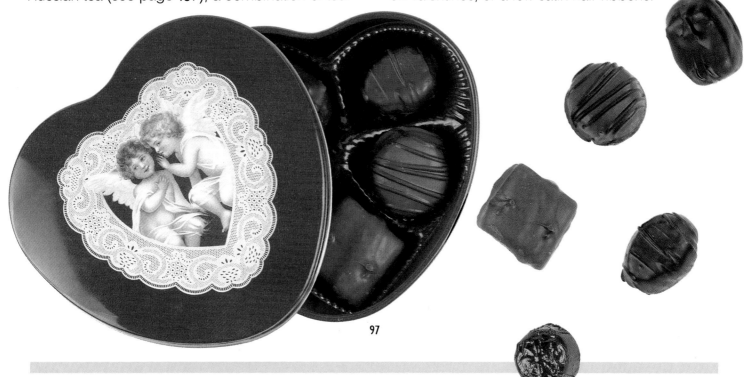

WOVEN HEART

The best paper to use for these hearts is a fairly sturdy, close-grained art paper that isn't too stiff. Regular construction paper is too pulpy and tears easily as you work. 1) Cut rectangles, 2½ inches by 9 inches, one red and one white. Fold each in half to measure 2½ by 4½ inches, making clean, sharp folds. 2) Cut three slits in each, as shown. The strips formed by these cuts need to be perfectly even. Round the other end, as shown. 3) Using the diagram as a guide, weave the paper strips together. The only trick is to open each fold alternately and pass the folded strips through the fold in the opposite color. Insert white loop A through red loop D. Then slip it *around* loop C, through loop B and around loop A. Weave white loop B around red loop D, through loop C, around loop B, through loop A. Continue until all the loops are woven. Don't be discouraged if the paper rips while you are still learning. If the paper seems too stiff and difficult, you can cheat a little by widening the slits just slightly with sharp scissors or a single-edged razorblade. This allows you just a little more space and makes weaving easier. You can also make these hearts with stiff felt, which is easier to weave, but paper is the traditional material.

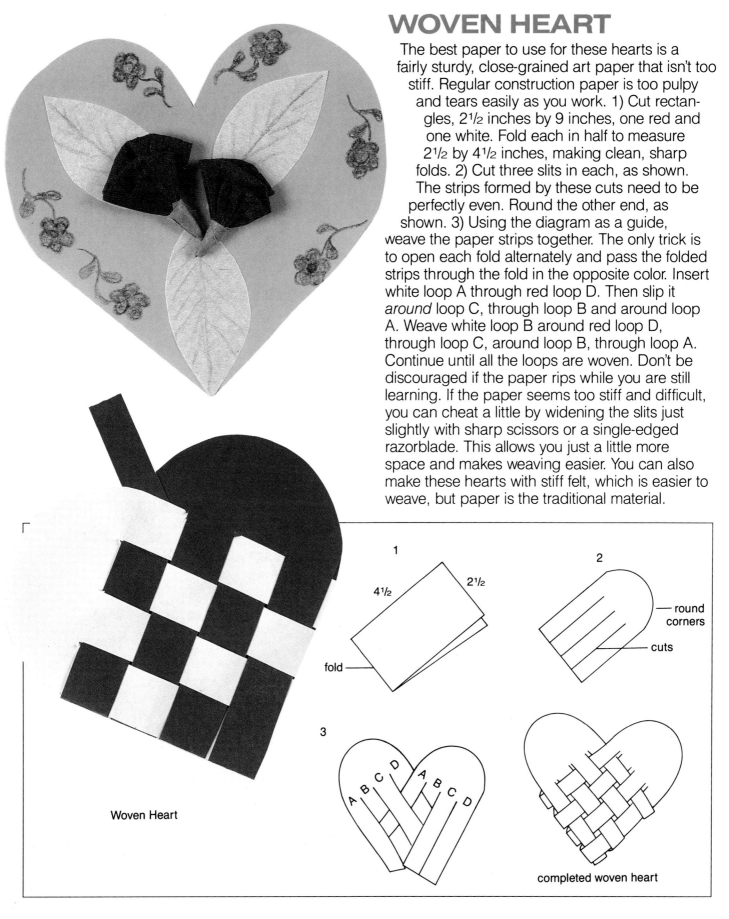

Woven Heart

1

4½   2½

fold

2

round corners

cuts

3

A B C D   A B C D

completed woven heart

VALENTINE CAKE

Finish off the celebration with a lace-topped cake. Frost either a round or heart-shaped cake very smoothly with red or deep pink icing. Using your cake pan as a pattern, cut a piece of waxed paper the exact size and shape of the top of the cake. Fold this pattern and cut a lacy snowflake from it. You can also cut a circle into several hearts, then cut lacy patterns into the edges of each. Or, you can purchase cake stencils from cake decorating suppliers. If you can find paper doilies without solid centers, they'll also work well.

Set the hearts, snowflake, stencil or doily lightly on the iced cake. Put about 1/2 cup of confectioners' sugar in a sifter. Hold it above the cake and tap its sides lightly, gently squeezing the sifter so that the whole cake gets a medium dusting of sugar. Gently blow the excess sugar from the paper so it won't slide off and ruin the design. Carefully lift the stencil from the cake. The result will be a stenciled pattern in white with a pink or red background. If you wish, you can further embellish this with silver shot.

If you don't have the time to make such an elaborate Valentine's Day cake, you can easily cut a round cake into a heart shape, frost it and decorate it with cinammon hearts and a nice message like, "Be Mine".

✓ **Party Theme:**   Magic and Illusion

✓ **Occasion:**   April Fools' Day

✓ **Ages:**   All ages

✓ **Invitations:**   Rabbit-in-a-hat

✓ **Decorations:**   Black and white, top hats

✓ **Refreshments:**   General

✓ **Cake:**   A chocolate cake will disappear like magic!

✓ **Favors and Prizes:**   Small tricks, magicians' wands

✓ **Games and Activities:**   Magic show

✓ **Special Requirements:**   None

April Fools' Party

While it is rarely considered an occasion for a party, this day is fun to observe as long as all the tricks and jokes are harmless ones that don't cause hurt feelings. Kids love to be the target of a fun trick just as much as they like to be the perpetrator.

Invitations to a magic party can be cut in the shape of a black top hat. When these are opened they can have a white rabbit inside with the information written on it.

This is a good occasion for a treasure hunt— one with tricks in the clues or a real April Fool involved in the prize. One mother did this by announcing just before the treasure hunt began, that the cake that had been sitting on the back-porch table was missing. "Someone must have stolen it!" she said. The children were crushed— what's a party without a cake?

"Let's go ahead with the treasure hunt and I'll try to think of something," suggested the mother, looking distraught. Caught up in the fun of the hunt, the children moved from clue to clue until they found the prize—a beautifully decorated cake hidden in the pantry. No one was more surprised than the daughter whose party it was, and everyone was delighted to have been taken in by the trick.

Magic is perfect entertainment for an April Fools' Party. Many areas have professional magicians who will come to birthday parties and do shows. They are listed in the Yellow Pages. Your local party store may also have a list.

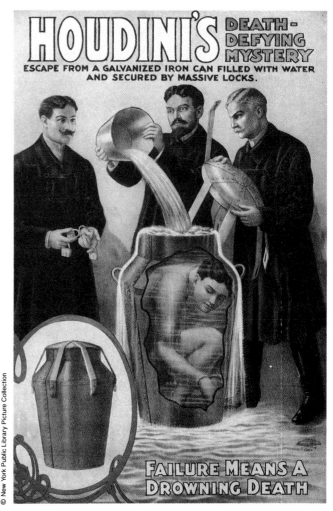

Houdini was the ultimate trickster.

If you cannot find a magician, why not be the magician yourself or let an older brother or sister entertain everyone with a short show? Look in the library for a magic book. Those designed for children will have easy tricks that use common household items.

Your decorations can center around magic. Inexpensive top hats are available in toy stores, and make great party favors. Toy stores also have good magic tricks to use as favors, such as trick boxes that make coins disappear. Older children would enjoy performing these tricks at an impromptu magic show where each had a turn being the magician.

There are other tricks that you can play on the party-goers. Imagine the surprise of cutting into a birthday cake made of foam, or of unwrapping a box that contains another wrapped box that contains another until at last the gift is found in the smallest box.

After you have amazed the guests with a magic show, you might be prepared to show how one or two tricks are done and provide the materials as party favors so children can go home and amaze their families. Magic wands—essential for any magician—are easily made by cutting 12-inch lengths of dowel and dipping them in shiny black paint.

Make sure that Merlin and his magic wand are at your party, at least in spirit. Use a rabbit-in-a-hat (right) to invite your guests.

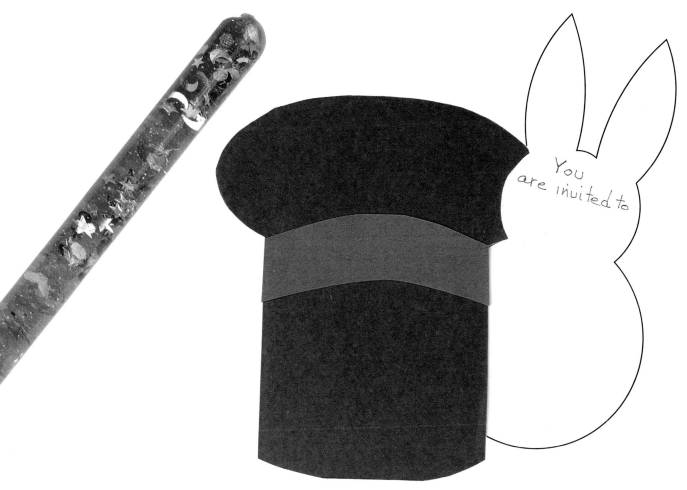

You are invited to

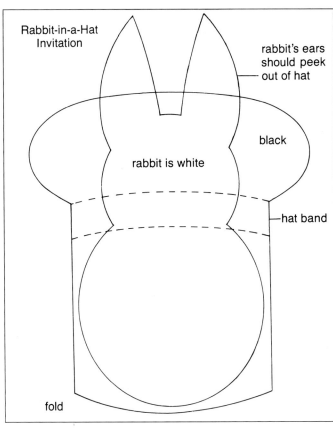

Rabbit-in-a-Hat Invitation

rabbit's ears should peek out of hat

black

rabbit is white

hat band

fold

RABBIT-IN-A-HAT INVITATION

Making invitations that do something surprising is not only fun for you, but also gives the guests a hint of the excitement that's in store. What could be a better clue to a party full of magic than a white rabbit inside a hat?

First find fairly square envelopes, such as those used for wedding invitations. You can buy these at stationers or from printers. Draw a pattern of a silhouette of a top hat that will fit inside the envelopes. Fold a piece of black construction paper in half. Trace the hat pattern onto the folded paper so that the brim of the hat is at the fold. Cut it out. Paste a hat band made of red construction paper on the hat. Cut one hat for each guest.

Using the illustration as a guide, draw a rabbit pattern and use it to cut one rabbit out of white construction paper for each invitation. Write the information on the rabbits and put them inside the hats so their ears stick out above the top hat, but still fit in the envelopes. Put the hats in the envelopes and mail them.

✓ **P**arty **T**heme: Doll Party

✓ **O**ccasion: Birthday

✓ **A**ges: 3 to 8

✓ **I**nvitations: Paper dolls

✓ **D**ecorations: Elegant, with lace and flowers

✓ **R**efreshments: Finger sandwiches, fancy cookies

✓ **C**ake: Frosted with flowers

✓ **F**avors and **P**rizes: Hair ribbons for guests, with matching ones for dolls, paper dolls

✓ **G**ames and **A**ctivities: Playing with dolls or paper dolls, paper-doll spiderwebs

✓ **S**pecial **R**equirements: None

Doll Party

Best for girls three-to-eight-years old, the doll party may also be appropriate for some older children, if dolls still capture their imaginations.

The dreamiest doll party of all is a Ladies' Tea Party. Elegance is the key to this party.

The tea table should be decorated with a bouquet of flowers and a china tea service. Make little tea napkins out of 9-inch squares of flowered fabric with the edges unraveled to form a fringe. Paper doilies can be used under the cookies on plates. If possible, there should be chairs for the dolls as well as the girls.

Invitations should be written in script on delicate pink cards or paper-doll invitations. Each guest is invited to bring a favorite doll, and fancy dress should be mentioned.

Serve Russian tea, made with tea and fruit juices, hot chocolate or iced tea, made with ginger ale and fruit juice and garnished with mint sprigs. Finger sandwiches and dainty cookies would be perfect to serve.

This occasion calls for an elegant cake decorated with flowers, or in the shape of a doll. You should act as a maid or butler, serving the food, clearing the dishes away and replenishing the tea, sandwiches and cookies.

Children love to invite dolls to their parties—sometimes dolls are the most important guests of all!

PAPER-DOLL INVITATIONS

The same fold-and-cut process that you used to make long strings of paper dolls when you were a child can be used to make unusual party invitations. By folding a strip of origami paper or other thin colored paper into an accordion, and then cutting a design from the folded sections, you can make a repeating design that fits very well onto a folded invitation the size of a small standard envelope.

Cut out a 6-by-1½-inch strip of paper. Fold it in half, then in thirds. These last folds should be accordion style, and all the edges should be even. Trace the doll pattern you want onto a thin sheet of paper and cut it out. Then place the pattern on the folded paper and cut around it. Be sure to leave a portion at each edge uncut so the dolls will hold together. Unfold it carefully and trim away any rough spots.

Cut a piece of art paper or light card stock to 6 inches by 6½ inches and fold it in half to become 6 inches by 3¼ inches. Using a little glue or spray adhesive, attach the cutouts to the front of the card. Write the necessary information inside.

TEA NAPKINS

Half a yard of gingham or calico fabric 45 inches wide will make ten tea-sized napkins. Measuring carefully, cut it into ten 9-inch squares, removing both selvages. Be sure edges are cut straight. With the point of a large needle, separate a few threads from one edge and ravel them out, continuing until you have a fringe about ¼ inch wide. Repeat on each side.

RUSSIAN TEA

1 pot brewed tea • ½ cup pineapple juice for each cup of tea • ½ cup orange juice for each cup of tea • Sugar, if desired • Lemon and orange slices, halved

Measure tea, and pour it into a saucepan. Add juices. Heat mixture almost to boiling. Pour it into a warmed teapot. Serve hot. Have the guests add sugar at the table if they want sweeter tea. Garnish with lemon and orange slices.

✓ **P**arty **T**heme: Graduation

✓ **O**ccasion: Graduation from kindergarten or grade school

✓ **A**ges: Kindergarten to 12

✓ **I**nvitations: Fancy script on parchment, rolled and tied in ribbons of school colors

✓ **D**ecorations: School colors, mortar boards

✓ **R**efreshments: Buffet luncheon, dinner or just desserts

✓ **C**ake: Frosted in school colors or blue and white

✓ **F**avors and **P**rizes: Not needed

✓ **G**ames and **A**ctivities: Not needed

✓ **S**pecial **R**equirements: None

Graduation Party

When your child graduates from any level of kindergarten or elementary school, he or she will be enormously proud of the accomplishment, and look forward to the next step. A graduation party with all the trappings will make it clear that you, too, see this as an important event.

Decorate the party with grown-up graduation symbols—mortarboards, rolled diplomas, class and school colors or just the colors blue and white. This gives the party the air of a high school or college commencement—big stuff for little people.

Decorate the party room and the buffet table with streamers. Use napkins and paper plates with graduation designs, or use a tablecloth in one of the school colors and paper goods in the other or use the traditional blue and white color scheme.

Since grandparents or other adults will probably be around, it's appropriate to host a luncheon following the graduation. If the graduation is at a different time of day, it can be preceded by a luncheon or dinner party or followed by a simple dessert party. You might wish to invite the parents and special guests of one of your child's classmates to join you.

The cake can be baked in the shape of the class year (see Appendix for source of number-shaped cake pans) or it can be a standard shape with little figures of graduates in caps and gowns on the top.

Invitations can be written on parchment-like stationery. Or send impressive diploma invitations.

© Jim Whitmer

DIPLOMA INVITATION

Use sheets of ivory parchment paper, available at art or stationery shops that carry calligraphy supplies. The paper comes in pads with guide sheets so you can keep your writing in neat, perfect lines.

Using a calligraphy pen (called a chisel point) write the invitation in flowing script—or as close as you can come to it. Practice first on regular paper.

Roll the invitations, tie them with a narrow blue ribbon and make a small bow. Send these in mailing tubes, or if you're inviting guests you see frequently, deliver them by hand.

APPENDIX

Mail Order and Retail Sources

Boycans
P.O. Box 897
Sharon, PA 16146
(412) 346-6181 (mail order)
Feathers, party favors

Childcraft
20 Kilmer Road
P.O. Box 500
Edison, NJ 08818
(800) 367-3255 (mail order)
Supplies, decorations, party favors

Cuddle Toy Factory Store
P.O. Drawer D
Keene, NH 03431
(603) 352-3414 (mail order)
Toys

Gettinger Feather Corporation
16 West 36th Street
New York, NY 10018
(212) 695-9470
(mail order and retail)
All sorts of feathers

Hank Lee's Magic Factory
P.O. Box 789
Medford, MA 02155 (mail order)
24 Lincoln Street
Boston, MA 02111
(617) 482-8749 (retail)
Magic show supplies

Klig's Kites
9600 North King's Highway
Myrtle Beach, NC 29572
(800) 333-5944
(mail order and retail)
Kites, small party favors

La Piñata
2 Patio Market, Old Town
Alburquerque, NM 87104
(505) 242-2400
(mail order and retail)
All sizes and types of piñatas

Lillian Vernon
510 South Fulton Avenue
Mount Vernon, NY 10550
(914) 633-6400 (mail order)
546 Main Street
New Rochelle, NY 10801
(914) 636-4294 (retail)
Small party favors

Maid of Scandinavia
3244 Raleigh Avenue
Minneapolis, MN 55416
(612) 927-7996
(mail order and retail)
Novelty cake pans, decorations, paper plates and napkins

Metropolitan Museum of Art
Children's Shop
82nd Street and Fifth Avenue
New York, NY 10028
(212) 879-5500 x2926
(mail order and retail)
Party favors, masks

Museum of Natural History
Junior Shop
Central Park West and 79th Street
New York, NY 10024
(212) 769-4746
(mail order and retail)
Party favors, dinosaur paraphernalia

The Nature Company
P.O. Box 2310
Berkeley, CA 94702
(800) 227-1114 (mail order)
8 Fulton
South Street Seaport
New York, NY 10038
(212) 422-8510 (retail)
740 Hearst Street
Berkeley, CA 94702
(415) 524-9052 (retail)
Party supplies, decorations, masks

Paradise Products
P.O. Box 568
El Cerrito, CA 94530
(415) 524-8300 (mail order and retail)
Party supplies, decorations

Toy Balloon Corporation
204 East 38th Street
New York, NY 10016
(212) 682-3803
(mail order and retail)
All kinds of balloons

INDEX

Pages 53/54 illustration by
Robert Frank/Melissa Turk
& The Artist Network

All uncredited silhouettes by
Christopher Bain